Squares and fo

Rome

Francesca Castria Marchetti

Electa

Summary

**From Piazza del Popolo
to Piazza di Spagna**

10 Piazza del Popolo
16 Fountain of Julius III
17 Fountain of the Babuino
17 Fountain of the Artists
18 Piazza di Spagna
21 Fountain of San Sebastianello
21 Fountain of Villa Medici

Campo Marzio

22 Piazza Augusto Imperatore
25 Fountain of the Botticella
26 Fountain of the Navigators
26 Fountain of Piazza Nicosia
27 Piazza San Lorenzo in Lucina
28 Piazza Montecitorio
29 Piazza di Pietra
30 Piazza Colonna

**From Trevi Fountain
to Piazza della Repubblica**

32 Trevi Fountain
36 Piazza del Quirinale
38 The Four Fountains
40 Triton Fountain
42 Fountain of the Bees
43 Fountain of Moses
44 Fountain of the Naiads

Pages 2-3,
*Gian Lorenzo Bernini,
Fountain of the Four Rivers
in Piazza Navona, 1648-1651.*

Pages 4-5,
*Nicola Salvi, Giuseppe
Pannini, Trevi Fountain,
1732-1762.*

Pages 6-7,
*Gian Lorenzo Bernini,
St. Peter's Square, 1667,
aerial view.*

Rione Pigna
48 Piazza della Rotonda
52 Piazza della Minerva
53 Fountain of Via Santo Stefano del Cacco
54 Fountain of the Porter
55 Piazza Sant'Ignazio

Piazza Navona
56 Piazza Navona
62 Fountain of Piazzetta di San Simeone
63 Piazza Sant'Eustachio
63 Fountain of the Books
64 Piazza Sant'Andrea della Valle
65 Tureen Fountain

Campo de' Fiori
and Rione Sant'Angelo
66 Campo de' Fiori
67 Fountain of the Mask
68 Piazza Farnese
70 Fountain of the Monte di Pietà
70 Fountain of Piazza Cairoli
71 Piazza Campitelli
72 Fountain of the Turtles
74 Fountain of Piazza delle Cinque Scole

Aventino
76 Piazza della Bocca della Verità
78 Drinking trough on Lungotevere
   Aventino
79 Fountain of the Mask of Santa Sabina
80 Fountain of Sant'Alessio
81 Fountain of the Amphorae

Campidoglio and Piazza Venezia
82 Fountain of Piazza d'Aracoeli
83 Campidoglio
90 Piazza Venezia

Celio and Esquilino
94 Piazza del Colosseo
98 Piazza Madonna dei Monti
99 Piazza Santa Maria Maggiore
102 Piazza Vittorio Emanuele II
104 Piazza San Giovanni in Laterano
107 Fountain of the Navicella

Gianicolo and Trastevere
108 Fountain of the Acqua Paola
110 Fountain of Ponte Sisto
111 Fountain of Piazza Mastai
112 Fountain of the Prigione
114 Fountain of Piazza Santa Maria
   in Trastevere
116 Piazza Giuseppe Gioacchino Belli

St. Peter's Square
118 St. Peter's Square
123 Fountain of the Pigna
123 Fountain of the Galera
124 Fountains of Via della Conciliazione

City map
pages 126-127

Piazza del Popolo

One of the most spectacular squares in Rome, it owes its appearance to two great architects, Gian Lorenzo Bernini and Giuseppe Valadier, the leading lights of two important periods from the viewpoint of city planning, the Baroque and the Neoclassical. At the end of the 16th century the square, which greets the visitor arriving in the city from the north, was fairly austere, embellished solely by the Church of Santa Maria del Popolo, rebuilt under Sixtus IV Della Rovere (1471-1484), and a fountain created by Giacomo Della Porta. Ten years later Pope Sixtus V Peretti (1585-1590) set up the Flaminio obelisk, found broken into pieces in the Circus Maximus, alongside the fountain. The following century Alexander VII Chigi (1655-1667) carried out a restyling of the square to coincide with the arrival in Rome of Queen Christina of Sweden, entrusting Bernini with the renovation of the Porta del Popolo and to Carlo Rainaldi the construction of twin churches on the opposite side of the square, Santa Maria in Montesanto and Santa Maria dei Miracoli. The work was interrupted on Alexander VII's death and then resumed in 1673 thanks to the financial support of Cardinal Gastaldi, who put Carlo Fontana and Gian Lorenzo Bernini in charge of the project. Rainaldi's design of two identical churches was modified by Bernini to suit the two different sites: Santa Maria in Montesanto was given an elliptical plan with a dodecagonal dome, while Santa Maria dei Miracoli was circular with an octagonal dome. Special technical stratagems were employed, however, to make the two churches look identical when seen from the square. No significant interventions were carried out in the 18th century, and it was not until the beginning of the 19th that Giuseppe Valadier's layout of the square in a Neoclassical style gave Piazza del Popolo its definitive appearance, the product of a happy blend of architecture and nature.

Giuseppe Valadier, Piazza del Popolo, 1816-1824.

Carlo Rainaldi, Churches of Santa Maria in Montesanto and Santa Maria dei Miracoli in Piazza del Popolo, 1679 and 1681.

Porta del Popolo, front on Piazzale Flaminio.

*Giuseppe Valadier,
Fountain
of the Egyptian
lions at the base
of the Flaminian
obelisk in
Piazza del Popolo
(see detail below)
and the Fountain
of the goddess
Roma in the
background,
1823.*

Giuseppe Valadier's Neoclassical Design

The layout of Piazza del Popolo and the Pincio hill occupied Valadier for many years, from the first project of 1793 until its completion in 1824, and answered to the need to connect the formerly more densely populated area close to the Tiber with the Pincio hill. So the trapezoidal square was extended at the sides with two hemicycles, in an extraordinary example of Neoclassical city planning. In each of the two semicircles Valadier placed a travertine fountain with a basin in the form of a shell, each surmounted by a sculptural group carved by Giovanni Ceccarini in 1823 to a design by Valadier himself: on the Pincio side we see the goddess Roma flanked by the Tiber and the Aniene, while on the side near the river Neptune stands between two tritons reining in dolphins.

At the center of the square, following the removal of Della Porta's fountain, which had always been regarded as inadequate, Valadier set the obelisk on top of a broad quadrangular base with five steps. On the summit of truncated stepped pyramids at its sides he placed four white marble lions, from whose mouths jets of water fan out into circular travertine basins underneath.

Giuseppe Valadier and Giovanni Ceccarini, Fountain of Neptune in Piazza del Popolo, whole and detail, 1823.

Pages 14-15, *Giuseppe Valadier and Giovanni Ceccarini, Fountain of the goddess Roma in Piazza del Popolo, 1823.*

Fountain of Julius III

In 1553 Pope Julius III Ciocchi del Monte (1550-1555) had a large fountain, fed by the Acqua Vergine, built by the architect Bartolomeo Ammannati on the Via Flaminia outside Porta del Popolo, not far from his villa. The fountain, which was to undergo major alterations over the course of time, was originally made up of a granite basin surmounted by an ancient head of Apollo from whose mouth flowed the water, set in the middle of an elegant architectural front: two Corinthian columns of marble supported the architrave with a tympanum, while statues of Felicity and Abundance were housed in two large quadrangular niches at the sides; above the tympanum stood the statue of Neptune flanked by those of Minerva and Roma.

A few years later Pope Pius IV de' Medici (1560-1565) decided to build his palace on the Via Flaminia, incorporating the fountain. On the occasion it was raised by the addition of a second tier, designed by the architect Pirro Ligorio. At the same time the statues above the tympanum were removed, as well perhaps as the ones in the niches at the sides. The palace with the annexed fountain was donated by the pope to his nephew, Cardinal Carlo Borromeo, who in turn gave it to his sister Anna, on the occasion of her marriage to Fabrizio Colonna in 1566.

The last and regrettable modifications were made at the beginning of the 17th century by Filippo Colonna, PALIANI DUX MAG NEAPOL REGNI COMESTABILIS (Duke of Paliano, Grand Constable of the Kingdom of Naples), as the inscription set above the fountain tells us. He replaced the fine ancient head of Apollo with a mediocre head of an old man, flanked by two dolphins and topped by the coat of arms of the Colonna family. Owing to the heavy alterations, the architectural complex of Pope Julius III that we see today differs greatly from Ammannati's grandiose design, yet it retains its fascination and nobility.

Bartolomeo Ammannati, Fountain of Julius III in Via Flaminia, 1553.

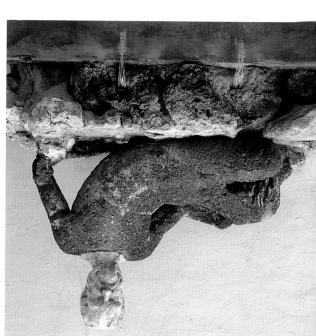

Fountain of the Babuino in Via del Babuino. 1580.

Pietro Lombardi, Fountain of the Artists in Via Margutta. 1927.

Pages 18-19, Piazza di Spagna and Piazza Mignanelli in the background.

Fountain of the Babuino

The Fountain of the Sileno, renamed by the Roman people Fountain of the Babuino was commissioned by Alessandro Grandi, owner of land and houses along what was then called Via Paolina, now Via del Babuino. Grandi, who had financed the reconstruction of the ancient Roman Acqua Vergine aqueduct, was granted a three-ounce flow of that water by the pope in 1580, along with the obligation to build a public fountain. The ounce was a unit of measurement equal to a flow of water varying between 16 and 18 liters per second.

The fountain, composed of a statue of a reclining Silenus above a granite basin from the time of ancient Rome, was originally set in a façade with niches built onto Grandi's palace. In 1738, with the construction of Palazzo Boncompagni Ludovisi, now Cerasi, the fountain was moved to a new niche, set in the façade of the new building and framed by two pilaster strips and an architrave, on which a pair of dolphins carved from travertine support a small balcony. Dismantled in 1877 because it was impeding traffic, the statue was set up in the courtyard of Palazzo Cerasi while the basin was borrowed by the drinking trough on the Via Flaminia, opposite the Fountain of Julius III. There it stayed until 1965 when, at the heartfelt request of the citizens of Rome, the Fountain of the Babuino was reassembled, but on the opposite side of the street, next to the Church of Sant'Atanasio dei Greci.

Fountain of the Artists

The unusual Fountain of the Artists, created in 1927 by the architect Pietro Lombardi, consists of a triangular base inserted in a marble arch and decorated with an allegorical ensemble of easels, palettes, compasses and other instruments symbolizing the activity that used to characterize Via Margutta, once inhabited by artists but now filled with antique stores.

Spanish Steps

In the 17th and 18th century the Scalinata di Trinità dei Monti, known in English as the "Spanish Steps", was the nodal point of the square which faced the seats of the two great powers that dominated pontifical politics: France on the Pincio hill with the Church of Trinità dei Monti, founded by the French in 1585, and the Villa Medici that from 1803 housed the Academy of France, founded by Louis XIV in 1666, and Spain with the Spanish Embassy to the Holy See. Planned as early as the middle of the 17th century, when Cardinal Mazarin

Piazza di Spagna

Piazza di Spagna is one of the most celebrated squares in the world, filled at every hour of the day by tourists and locals, who like to meet there on Saturdays before strolling down Via Condotti, formerly Via Trinitatis, with its stores of worldwide fame. Laid out in the shape of a butterfly, the piazza is split into two triangles whose vertices overlap at the center, at the point where Bernini's fountain stands. Onto the northern triangle face 18th-century townhouses to which an extra story was added in the 19th, painted in shades of yellow ocher and rust red, while the southern triangle is surrounded by 17th-century buildings like Palazzo di Spagna, seat of the Spanish Embassy to the Holy See since 1647. Opposite it stands the column of the Immaculate Conception, a monument inaugurated in 1856 to celebrate the dogma proclaimed by Pius IX Mastai Ferretti (1846-1878). The column, made of cipollino marble and dating from the 1st century, was found in Campo Marzio in 1777. It was set on an octagonal base decorated with statues of the prophets Moses, Isaiah, Ezekiel and David, and surmounted by a bronze statue of the Virgin. The square is closed by the Palazzo di Propaganda Fide, begun by Gian Lorenzo Bernini and finished in 1662 by Francesco Borromini with the splendid western façade animated by a succession of concave and convex surfaces.

Fountain of the Barcaccia

In 1626 Urban VIII Barberini (1623-1644) commissioned a fountain to be set at the foot of the planned flight of steps leading to Trinità dei Monti to Pietro Bernini, whom he had appointed architect of the Acqua Vergine. Pietro came up with a very bold design that broke with traditional schemes, availing himself of the precious collaboration of his son Gian Lorenzo, especially for the sculptural decoration. In contrast to Della Porta's severe and repetitive fountains, in which the water is scarcely visible and stone predominates, Bernini chose to do without basins and shells, allowing the water to flow freely inside and outside the fanciful boat. The fountain was baptized the "barcaccia," or "old tub" by the Romans, but this apparently derogatory name was in reality that of a riverboat used in the 17th century to bring cargoes in and out of the Port of Ripetta. Tradition has it that the sculptor was inspired by the story of a boat that had come to grief during the flooding of the Tiber in 1598, running aground at the foot of the Pincio. Immersed in an oval basin, the travertine boat with water gushing from all sides looks really as if it is about to sink. And yet the fountain does not present the normal characteristics of a boat: instead of a bow and stern, it has two identical ends of elongated shape that are decorated with the Sun, symbol of the Barberini family, blowing a jet of water. The basin is located below the level of the ground to compensate for the low pressure of the Acqua Vergine in the area, too close to the cisterns at the foot of the Rampa di San Sebastianello.

asked his agent in Rome to come up with a design for a staircase to replace the steep paths that ran up and down the grassy slope of the Pincio, it was not until the papacy of Innocent XIII Conti (1721-1724) that its construction was entrusted to Francesco De Sanctis. In De Sanctis's design the influence of the Port of Ripetta, built by Alessandro Specchi twenty years earlier, is evident. However, instead of the systematic symmetry of the steps at Ripetta, dictated by the geometric shape of the oval square onto which the Church of San Gerolamo faces, De Sanctis designed a structure that, through the

convexity and concavity of its surfaces, fuses the irregularity and asymmetry of the surrounding architectural elements into a coherent organism. Like the one in the port, the staircase on Piazza di Spagna utilizes a combination of several flights that go along with the natural slope in a movement of extraordinary elegance.

At the sides of the Spanish Steps the buildings facing onto the square, also designed by De Sanctis, act as architectural wings to the imposing scene, which reaches the height of its splendor in spring, when the steps are adorned with azaleas.

From Piazza del Popolo to Piazza di Spagna

Annibale Lippi,
Fountain
of Villa Medici,
1587.

Fountain of
San Sebastianello,
c. 1570.

and the Spanish
Steps (Francesco
De Sanctis,
1723-1726).

Piazza di Spagna
with the Fountain
of the Baraccia
(Pietro and Gian
Lorenzo Bernini,
1626-1629)

Fountain of Villa Medici

In front of the main entrance of Villa Medici, shaded by the holm oaks of the avenue, stands this fountain, very dear to the Romans, around which the most fanciful stories have grown up. One of them holds that the ball of stone at the center of the basin, from which the water gushes, is a cannonball that was fired by Queen Christina of Sweden from Castel Sant'Angelo in 1655 at Villa Medici, where her favorite, the French painter Charles Errard, was staying. Built in 1472 for Cardinal Ricci di Montepulciano by the architect Annibale Lippi, the villa was purchased four years later by Cardinal Ferdinando de' Medici. In 1587, after superintending the work of bringing the Acqua Felice to Rome, he was granted a flow of several ounces of the water carried by the aqueduct by Sixtus V. The same year Cardinal de' Medici acquired an old basin of red granite from the Friars of San Salvatore in Lauro and used it to build the fountain. Set on top of a broad octagonal base, it is located at the center of a pool, also octagonal in shape, hollowed out of the ground at the level of the road: the water spurts from the ball into the basin, from where it spills over into the pool underneath.

Fountain of San Sebastianello

Halfway up the steep slope of the Rampa di San Sebastianello, the fountain of the same name is located in a niche set in the retaining wall of Viale di Trinità dei Monti. The fountain is made up of an ancient sarcophagus, from which the water spurts through three holes into the pool beneath. The sarcophagus, which has a portrait of the dead woman it used to contain on the front, between two images of the Good Shepherd, is one of many such caskets that have been turned into fountains: an exchange of functions that turns on its head a custom common in the Middle Ages, when basins from ancient Roman baths were used to bury martyrs and saints. The fountain is fed by the Acqua Vergine. Entering the city from the north, the aqueduct ends at the Pincio: at the foot of Rampa di San Sebastianello stand two cisterns to collect the water, from which pipes run for a distance of five kilometers, supplying the fountains of Piazza del Popolo, Piazza Colonna and Piazza Venezia.

Piazza Augusto Imperatore

A place currently at the center of bitter disputes over the new museum for the Ara Pacis, designed by the architect Richard Meier, Piazza Augusto Imperatore in the Republican era was an area of farmland dedicated to Mars, which is why the district was called Campus Martius. In the imperial age the explosive growth of the city had induced Augustus to urbanize the area of Campo Marzio, and its use for predominantly public purposes persisted until the end of the 15th century, when the urbanization of the area between Via del Corso and the Tiber and the commercial landing place on the river, where Piazza Augusto Imperatore is now located, laid the foundations for the successive Baroque development of the district.

The construction of the Port of Ripetta at the beginning of the 18th century led to the emergence of a dense urban fabric, but this was cancelled out by the heavy modifications made from the end of the 19th century onward: from the construction of the embankments of the Tiber, with the consequent destruction of the port, to the monumental layout of Piazza Augusto Imperatore, carried out by Vittorio Morpurgo between 1937 and 1940. Morpurgo cleared the area around the mausoleum of Augustus, making it the center of a square bounded by monumental buildings with high porticoes, while on the side of the square facing the Tiber he built a simple pavilion of marble and glass to house the *Ara Pacis Augustae*, uncovered in the nearby Piazza di San Lorenzo in Lucina.

Mausoleum of Augustus

Built by Augustus in 28 BC as a tomb for himself and his descendants, the monument had a circular structure with a diameter of 87 meters. The entrance faced south and was flanked by two obelisks reaching a height of 14.80 meters, one of which is now in Piazza del Quirinale and the other in Piazza dell'Esquilino. The spaces inside were divided up into concentric circles centering on a 44-meter-high cylindrical pillar that supported the statue of the emperor and housed Augustus's ashes. The first ring contained the graves of his wife Livia, sisters Octavia and Julia, with their husbands Mark Antony and Agrippa, nieces and nephews and other members of the family, while the other three rings were made up of a series of in-

accessible spaces that served to support the hanging garden above. Falling into ruin following the barbarian invasions of the 5th century, the mausoleum, of which only the lower part survives today, was put to a wide variety of uses over the centuries. The last of these was the famous Augusteo, a concert hall that was closed in 1936 when work began on laying out the square.

*Mausoleum
of Augustus
in Piazza Augusto
Imperatore,
28 BC.*

*Ara Pacis
in Piazza Augusto
Imperatore,
13-9 BC.*

Ara Pacis

Erected between 13 and 9 BC to celebrate the peace brought by Augustus to the empire, the Ara Pacis or "Altar of Peace," is one of the most important monuments of antiquity. Transported along the embankment of Lungotevere in 1938 at the time of the layout of Piazza Augusto Imperatore, the altar was originally located at the end of the sundial built by Augustus in Campo Marzio, on the site of what is now Piazza San Lorenzo in Lucina. However, all trace of the legendary monument was lost in late antiquity, and when the first fragments began to emerge in the foundations of Palazzo Fiano in the 16th century, along with the sundial and the obelisk of Psamtik II, their importance was not understood. The finds ended up in the hands of collectors and were dispersed among museums in Italy, the Vatican, Vienna and Paris. It was not until the end of the 19th century that further discoveries allowed German archeologists to identify the altar. This prompted Mussolini to order systematic excavations, and the monument was recovered in its entirety and then reconstructed on its present site.

The Ara Pacis consists of a rectangular enclosure (11.65 × 10.62 m), set on top of a base and accessible by two flights of steps leading to doors in each of the long sides, and the altar proper inside. The walls are decorated on the outside and inside with beautifully carved friezes and reliefs: the most important scene is the one representing the members of the imperial family arranged in hierarchic order on the outer surface of the north wall, while the interior is finely decorated with festoons of foliage and fruit above a palisade.

Fountain of the Botticella

Constructed for the Confraternita degli Osti, or Brotherhood of Innkeepers, which had its seat in the nearby Church of San Rocco, the small "Fountain of the Little Barrel" is dedicated to Pope Clement XIV Ganganelli (1769-1774), who had granted the confraternity a flow of a few ounces of the Acqua Vergine. Originally located on Palazzo Valdambrini, the fountain was moved in 1937 during the work on Piazza Augusto Imperatore: Palazzo Valdambrini and other buildings were demolished to clear space around the mausoleum of Augustus, while the two Churches of San Rocco and San Girolamo degli Schiavoni were also isolated and then linked by a bridge with a double fornix and the fountain in the middle. Set in a rectangular niche in a simple architectural façade, the fountain is composed of the valve of a shell from which protrudes the head of a young innkeeper wearing a beret. The water spurts from his mouth into a small circular basin standing on the rocks piled around the barrel, which receives the water through another rectangular basin that acts as a funnel. In many ways the composition recalls the Fountain of the Porter, dating from two centuries before: the barrel and the head of the young innkeeper with a beret are direct citations of it, but here the barrel is used to receive the water not to pour it.

Fountain of the Botticella in Largo San Rocco, 1774.

Alessandro Specchi, Fountain of the Navigators in Piazza del Porto di Ripetta, 1704.

Giacomo Della Porta and Giovanni Leminard, Fountain of Piazza Nicosia, 1572.

Fountain of the Navigators

Constructed to the design of Alessandro Specchi in 1704 along with the Port of Ripetta, under the pontificate of Clement XI Albani (1700-1721), the Fountain of the Navigators was intended to serve as a drinking place for porters and stevedores. Located at the top of the port's flight of steps, at the center of the exedra, the fountain was composed of an oval stone basin on which was set, on the side facing the Tiber, a rock supporting a large shell and two dolphins with their tails interlaced in the middle. The water gushed from the center of the rock and the mouths of the dolphins into the shell, from where it flowed into the basin underneath. Subsequently a wrought-iron lamp was placed on top of the fountain, to make the port more accessible at night time. When the port was demolished at the end of the 19th century to allow the construction of the embankments of the Tiber, the fountain was dismantled and placed in the municipal storehouses. In 1929 it was rebuilt, but without respecting the original design, and located on the southern side of the same square.

Fountain of Piazza Nicosia

The fountain, placed in Piazza Nicosia in 1950, was commissioned to Giacomo Della Porta in 1572 by Pope Gregory XIII Boncompagni (1572-1585) as a replacement for the ancient ruin called "Fontana del Trullo" in Piazza del Popolo. Della Porta took the Fountain of Santa Maria in Trastevere, the oldest of Rome's monumental fountains, as his model. But his creation proved inadequate, considering that Piazza del Popolo at the time was a vast empty space, in which the only structure was the Church of Santa Maria del Popolo. The fountain, fed by the Acqua Vergine, was composed of an octagonal marble basin, raised on two steps, with a baluster at the center adorned with four dolphins that supported an intermediate basin, decorated with two dragons and two eagles and surmounted by a small bowl. The basin was made by the French sculptor Giovanni Leminard from the base of a column of the Temple of Serapis on the Quirinal, while the sculptors Simone Moschino, Taddeo Landini, Giacobbe Silla Longhi and Egidio De Malines later carved four squatting tritons. However, these turned out to be too large for the dimensions of the fountain and were at once removed and placed on the Fountain of the Moor in Piazza Navona. In 1589, Pope Sixtus V Peretti made his own contribution to the fountain by adding an obelisk of red granite from the Circus Maximus. The last modifications were made by Giuseppe Valadier, who removed the fountain in 1823 as part of a general reorganization of the square. For a while it was placed in Piazza San Pietro in Montorio, and then ended up in storage. In 1950 the fountain was reconstructed in Piazza Nicosia, but all that is left of the original is the octagonal basin, while the central part is a restoration.

Piazza San Lorenzo in Lucina

The square occupies an area once filled with imperial buildings, from the Ara Pacis, discovered under Palazzo Firano in the 16th century, to Augustus's sundial, still being excavated in the courtyard of the adjoining Church of San Lorenzo in Lucina. The sundial is only one part of the *Horologium Augusti*, one of the technological and architectural wonders of ancient Rome. Along with the sundial, an area paved with travertine on which the months and the hours of the day were engraved, the clock comprised the Egyptian obelisk of Psamtik II, rebuilt at the end of the 18th century in the nearby Piazza Montecitorio, and even the Ara Pacis itself: on just one day of the year, September 23—Augustus's birthday—the obelisk cast a shadow that extended in a line all the way to the Ara Pacis, celebrating the greatness of the emperor, prince of peace. In addition, the vestiges of an ancient sanctuary, perhaps devoted to Juno Lucina, protectress of sick and pregnant women, were found under the Church of San Lorenzo in Lucina during excavations conducted at the end of

The Church of San Lorenzo in Lucina is one of the oldest places of worship in Christendom. Built in the 12th century and dedicated to St. Lawrence, whose relics—the gridiron and two ampullae of blood—are preserved in the first chapel, the church stands on the site of the ancient *titulus Lucinae*, documented since the 4th century. *Tituli* or *ecclesiae domesticae* were private houses used to hold Christian services before the religion was made legal. The church, which echoes the structure of the Roman house underneath, including its north-south orientation, has a Medieval façade preceded by a portico with six Roman columns with Ionian capitals, while the interior, originally divided into a nave and two aisles, was rebuilt in the 17th century, with the addition of chapels along the aisles, and restored in 1860 by the architect Andrea Busiri Vici and the painter Roberto Bompiani, who executed the

the last century. Support for this hypothesis can be seen in the presence of an old mosaic of the "Madonna of Health" above the high altar, still venerated today.

frescoes.

Piazza
San Lorenzo
in Lucina.

Piazza Montecitorio.

Piazza Montecitorio

On an artificial mound, a fact recorded in the name of the square, which comes from the Latin *Mons Accepto-rius*, stands the red granite obelisk of Psamtik II (594-589 BC), brought from Egypt by Augustus and original-ly set up in 10 BC to serve as the gnomon for a sundial in what is now Piazza San Lorenzo in Lucina. Its pres-ence on this site is documented until the 11th century, when it was demolished and covered by Medieval struc-tures. Although rediscovered at the beginning of the 16th century, in was not until 1792 that it was brought to the surface and restored by Giovanni Anthori, who gave it back its function as a sundial. The obelisk, 22 meters high, was set on a tall base and topped with a perforated bronze globe, through which the sun pro-jects its rays onto the pavement of the square, in which special flagstones mark the hours.

Behind the obelisk, on the longest side of the square, stands Palazzo Montecitorio, commissioned to Bernini in 1653 by Pope Innocent X Pamphilj (1644-1655). Interrupted by the pope's death, work on the building was resumed a few decades later by Carlo Fontana, who was commissioned by Pope Innocent XII Pignatelli (1691-1700) to turn it into the seat of the Curia Inno-cenziana. In 1871 it became the home of the Chamber of Deputies and in 1903 the architect Ernesto Basile be-gan to enlarge it, adding the parliamentary chamber in the area of the courtyard and the Art Nouveau façade on Piazza del Parlamento.

All that survives of Bernini's original design is the main façade on Piazza Montecitorio, punctuated by gigantic pilasters and characterized by its convex shape, with the central part projecting slightly. The entrance with three doorways and the belfry were added by Fontana.

Piazza di Pietra

The piazza takes its name (Stone Square) from the remains of the Temple of Hadrian, built by Antoninus Pius
in AD 145 and dedicated to his deified adoptive father
Hadrian. All that is left of the temple, which stood at the
center of a colonnaded square with its front facing east,
is the right-hand side with eleven Corinthian columns
of white marble, each 15 meters high and standing on a
tall base of blocks of travertine and peperino, along
with part of the cella. In 1695 Pope Innocent XII Pignatelli (1691-1700) entrusted Carlo Fontana, aided by
his son Francesco, with the construction of a building
to house the Dogana di Terra. Carlo Fontana realized a
large structure that incorporated the eleven columns
and the cornice, unintentionally creating a large, dark
mass that overshadowed the small square. The building, turned into the Stock Exchange at the end of the
19th century, was restored by Virginio Vespignani, who
altered the front, eliminating the Baroque decorations.

*Piazza di Pietra
with the columns
of the Temple
of Hadrian,
145 AD.*

Piazza Colonna

The only monumental square on the Corso, Piazza Colonna owes its name to the column of Marcus Aurelius, erected after the emperor's death in AD 180 to commemorate his victories over the Sarmatians and Marcomanni. The column, made of Luni marble, is 42 meters high and decorated with scenes of war, that wind in a spiral from the base up to the Doric capital. In 1588 it was restored by Domenico Fontana, who intervened on the base and the top, setting a bronze statue of St. Paul there in place of the one of the emperor, that had been lost during the Middle Ages. In the 16th century the column of Marcus Aurelius, flanked by modest little houses from the Medieval period, remained the distinguishing element of the square, which then included what is now Piazza di Pietra. From 1575 onward, with the interventions of Popes Gregory XIII Boncompagni (1572-1585) and Sixtus V Peretti (1585-1590), Piazza Colonna as-

sumed its present appearance, apart from the demolition of its eastern side in 1873 to permit the widening of the Corso and the construction of the Galleria Colonna, now named after Alberto Sordi. In 1575 Gregory XIII commissioned a fountain for the square to Giacomo Della Porta, who designed a basin of mixtilinear shape to be set against the column of Marcus Aurelius and adorned with the statue known popularly as Marforio, which at that time was located near the arch of Septimius Severus. All that was realized of this design was the basin, one of Della Porta's more natural creations, in portasanta marble and decorated solely with sixteen white marble lion heads arranged around the basin under its lip. Around 1580 work began on the construction di Palazzo Chigi, formerly Aldobrandini, on the northern side of the square, currently the seat of the presidency of the Council of Ministers. Finally, under Sixtus V, the small Medieval houses were demolished and replaced by noble

Column of Marcus Aurelius in Piazza Colonna, 180 AD.

Piazza Colonna and the fountain by Giacomo Della Porta, 1575.

townhouses, such as Palazzo Del Bufalo, later Ferrajoli, on the south side and Palazzo Wedekind on the west side, restored in the 19th century with the addition to the portico of eleven fluted columns with Ionian capitals, found at Veii during the excavations in 1812-1817. Around 1667 Pope Alexander VII Chigi (1655-1667) proposed realizing the grandiose project for the terminal point of the Acqua Vergine, i.e. the Trevi Fountain, in front of his palace on Piazza Colonna, transferring Della Porta's fountain to Piazza San Marco. The Chigi pope's plan came to nothing, leaving no trace except for the designs of Gian Lorenzo Bernini and Pietro da Cortona, and the only intervention carried out during his pontificate was a restoration of the fountain by Bernini. A later restoration by Alessandro Stocchi in 1830 entailed the replacement of the bowl at the center of the basin with a smaller and more modest one of white marble and the addition of two pairs of dolphins with interlaced tails inside shells on the short sides.

Nicola Salvi and Giuseppe Pannini.

Trevi Fountain in Piazza di Trevi, 1732-1762.

Trevi Fountain

The last spectacular creation of the Baroque in Rome, the Trevi Fountain, constitutes the endpoint of the Acqua Vergine, commenced by Nicola Salvi in 1732 and completed by Giuseppe Pannini in 1762. The Trevi Fountain is named after the place, a few kilometers from Rome, where the main sources of the Acqua Vergine are located. Constructed by Agrippa in 19 BC, the Roman Acqua Vergine aqueduct started from the *Ager Lucullanus* on the Via Tiburtina and ended in the city at a fountain in the vicinity of the Baths of Agrippa. A series of breakdowns of the aqueduct over the course of the Middle Ages led to the abandonment of the last part of its route and the choice of another fountain as its endpoint, identified as the original Trevi Fountain. This can be made out on the oldest plans of Rome, where it is represented alongside the city's main monuments. In the small and schematic plan of Rome frescoed by Taddeo di Bartolo in Siena in 1412, the Trevi Fountain is depicted with three basins set against the wall of a modest building. This simple structure was partially transformed by Leon Battista Alberti in 1453. Given the task of restoring and adorning the "decrepit duct of the Acqua Vergine" by Pope Nicholas V Parentucelli (1447-1455), he replaced the three basins with a single rectangular one. Further but not very significant modifications were made in the time of Sixtus IV Della Rovere (1471-1484), but the fountain, apart from the restoration carried out by Giacomo Della Porta in 1563, remained unaltered throughout the 16th century.

In the 17th century the works undertaken to redevelop the cramped surrounding area called for the opening of a new street, that would run past the fountain and require the demolition of part of it. The complete demolition of the fountain was carried out by Gian Lorenzo Bernini, who in 1640 was commissioned to build a new one by Urban VIII Barberini (1623-1644): with the work interrupted on the pope's death, all that was realized of Bernini's project was the base of a small exedra and two semicircular basins on the northern side of the square. The water spouted from the exedra through three mouths into the first basin, and then spilled over into the second, larger one. With the idea of creating the desired terminal fountain of the Acqua Vergine in Piazza di Trevi abandoned by later popes, nearly a century was to go by before Pope Clement XII Corsini (1730-1740) decided to resolve the longstanding problem in 1730, entrusting Nicola Salvi with the construction of the monumental fountain we see today. Salvi designed a rigid architectural setting with the motif of a triumphal arch in the middle, fusing reminiscences of Palladio and Bernini, which acts as a backdrop to the rockwork, central theme of the fountain. The result is a hallucinatory vision of nature, that conceals a carefully studied iconological structure, where water plays the role of connective tissue for the extraordinary spectacle created by the colossal allegorical figure of the Ocean, on a chariot drawn by seahorses and tritons.

Trevi Fountain, details.

Piazza del Quirinale

The Piazza del Quirinale occupies the top of the hill of the same name, facing west onto a panorama of the city. Housing the Temple of Serapis and the Baths of Constantine in the classical era, the area was progressively abandoned over the course of the Middle Ages, as its connections with the lower part of the city were poor. Fragments of the brick walls and the entablature of the Temple of Serapis, erected by Caracalla, survive in the gardens of Villa Colonna, on the south side of the square. Statues of the Dioscuri, two colossi over five meters high that are Imperial-era copies of Greek originals dating from the 5th century BC, used to adorn the entrance of Constantine's Baths, the last great public facility to be built in ancient Rome, whose remains are visible in the garden and basement of Palazzo Pallavicini Rospigliosi. The construction of the Palazzo del Quirinale at the end of the 16th century as a summer residence for the popes, made a reorganization of the square necessary, a task that Pope Sixtus V Peretti (1585-1590) entrusted to Domenico Fontana. Once he had completed the façade of the Palazzo del Quirinale, begun in 1573 by Martino Longhi the Elder and continued by Ottaviano Mascherino, Fontana moved the Dioscuri, originally located in front of the ruins of the ancient baths on the east side of the square, to the beginning of the Strada Pia, now Via del Quirinale, and set a fountain in front of them, fed by the Felice Aqueduct. It consists of a large octagonal basin with a baluster in the middle supporting a circular bowl, from which rises a jet of water. Subsequent interventions in the square concerned the Palazzo del Quirinale, which was enlarged by Carlo Maderno, who also designed the entrance (1615), where two columns support a tympanum decorated with statues of St. Peter and St. Paul, and by Gian Lorenzo Bernini, who livened up its compact façade with the circular tower on the left (1616) and the Loggia delle Benedizioni, above the doorway (1638). The square did not take on its definitive appearance until the time of Pope Pius VI Braschi (1775-1799), who in 1782 decided to erect the obelisk that had just been found in the vicinity of Augustus's mausoleum between the statues of the Dioscuri. The project, entrusted to Giovanni Antinori, entailed shifting the sculptural groups so that they faced the Quirinale at diverging angles, placing the obelisk in the middle and removing the fountain. Despite the pope's express declaration, that he intended to restore the old fountain, carved on the pedestal of the obelisk, many years went by and all trace of it was lost. Finally, in 1818, Pope Pius VII Chiaramonti (1800-1823) commissioned Raffaele Stern to make a new fountain, for which the large granite basin taken from the fountain in Campo Vaccino was utilized. The Palazzo del Quirinale is now the official residence of the president of the Republic, while the low building on the other side of the square that housed the stables of the Quirinale, commenced by Alessandro Specchi and completed by Ferdinando Fuga in 1730, is used to stage major exhibitions. Fuga also built the Palazzo della Consulta on the east side of the square, seat of the Constitutional Court since 1955.

Palazzo del Quirinale in Piazza del Quirinale, begun in 1573 and completed by Gian Lorenzo Bernini in 1638.

Domenico Fontana, Fountain of the Dioscuri in Piazza del Quirinale, 1588-1589.

The Four Fountains

The Four Fountains, built between 1588 and 1593, are a rare example of public fountains financed by a private individual. In 1588, the nobleman Muzio Mattei, who in 1580 had already funded the Fountain of the Turtles in front of his townhouse on Piazza Mattei, was granted a supply of water from the Acqua Felice by the pope for his palace with a garden on the Via Felice, now Palazzo del Drago, in exchange for the construction of three of the four fountains designed by Domenico Fontana for Pope Sixtus V Peretti (1585-1590). The fourth fountain was financed by a certain Giacomo Gridenzoni, in exchange for a flow of an ounce and a half of water granted by the pope in June 1593. The Four Fountains, located on the blunt-ed corners of the four buildings at the intersection of the old Strada Pia with the Via Felice (today Via delle Quattro Fontane and Via XX Settembre), emphasize a spectacular point, one of the most representative of Sixtus V's urban schemes: from the crossroads, in fact, it is possible to see Michelangelo's Porta Pia and the obelisks in Piazza dell'Esquilino, in Piazza del Quirinale and at Trinità dei Monti. Inside four niches, decorated with different natural scenes, four reclining allegorical figures in travertine are set above semicircular marble basins: the Tiber accompanied by the she-wolf, backing onto the Church of San Carlino, is followed in a clockwise direction by Fortitude leaning on a lion and with a goose or swan at her feet, Fidelity flanked by a dog, and the Nile with a lion.

Fountain of Tiber on the crossroads of the Four Fountains, by the Church of San Carlo, 1588.

Fountain of Fortitude, 1588.

*Fountain
of Fidelity
by Palazzo
Barberini,
1593.*

*Fountain of Nile
by Palazzo
del Drago,
1588.*

Triton Fountain

Commissioned to Gian Lorenzo Bernini in 1642 by Pope Urban VIII Barberini (1623-1644) for the square in front of his family palace, just completed by Bernini in collaboration with Francesco Borromini, the Triton Fountain is the artist's masterpiece in the genre. Four dolphins support a large open scallop shell with their tails and a triton seated on the shell blows water into the air through a conch held in his hands. Art historians have identified the models from which Bernini took his inspiration as two fountains in the Vatican Gardens: the Fountain of the Eagle dating from 1612 for the figure of the triton, and a fountain that has now vanished but which had been created a few years earlier by Nicolas Cordier, for the group of dolphins. However, while it is true that the Barberini triton displays a striking similarity to the figure carved by Stefano Maderno for the Fountain of the Eagle—the pose, the position of the arms and the conch into which he blows the water are identical—from the outset of his career Bernini had shown a unique ability to take a source of inspiration and rework it so profoundly, that the result took on a force and significance absent from the original. Sometimes he drew on a number of sources, and the skill with which he extrapolated new formal and iconographic associations from them is one of the principal reasons for his success.

Bernini abandoned the 16th-century model of the fountain, exemplified by Della Porta's creations: the artist adopted the technical device of lowering the basin, making the effect of the flowing water falling onto the mutable horizontal surface fully visible. In this way water, as a continually flowing element, was brought into the heart of the architectural setting, inextricably interlinking the potential movement of the sculpted form with the sense of movement created by the architectural structures and the actual motion of the water.

Gian Lorenzo Bernini, Triton Fountain in Piazza Barberini, 1642.

Fountain of the Bees

A small but extraordinary gem of sculpture, the Fountain of the Bees was originally created to serve as a drinking trough for horses near the monumental Triton Fountain. Carved by Bernini in 1644 and set on one corner of Palazzo Soderini, a building situated between Piazza Barberini and Via Sistina, it was removed in 1867 as it was blocking traffic, and abandoned in the municipal storehouses. When the decision was taken to salvage the fountain fifty years later, nothing was left of it but a fragment with the central bee. So the fountain was reconstructed by the sculptor Adolfo Apolloni and set up on the corner of Via Veneto and Via di San Basilio in 1916. Apolloni interpreted the model freely, placing the two valves of the open shell on a base of roughly hewn stones, so that the lower valve was no longer at ground level and the upper no longer set against a building, but isolated. Apolloni used gray travertine instead of white Luni marble and arranged the three bees, symbol of the Barberini family, from which the water spurts into the lower valve, on the hinge instead of the upper valve. This FONTE AD PUBLICUM URBIS ORNAMENTUM, as it is described in the dedication inscribed above, constitutes a small musical note in response to the massive Triton Fountain, where Bernini had explored the same theme of the open scallop shell, supported by four dolphins and surmounted by the imposing figure of the triton.

Gian Lorenzo Bernini, Fountain of the Bees in Via Veneto, 1644.

Fountain of Moses

Designed by Domenico Fontana in 1587 as a terminal for the Felice Aqueduct, the Fountain of Moses is composed of three large niches framed by four Ionian columns, that support the architrave and attic, surmounted by the papal coat of arms between two angels. A large inscription on the attic commemorates the action of Pope Sixtus V Peretti (1585-1590) in bringing to Rome the water from a source in the area of Pantano, an estate owned by the Colonna family at Zagarolo, which he renamed Acqua Felice after himself. In the lower part with the niches the water pours into basins flanked by Egyptian lions, originally located in Piazza della Rotonda, at the entrance of the Basilica of San Giovanni in Laterano. Removed from the fountain in the 19th century by Pope Gregory XVI Cappellari (1831-1846), and replaced with copies made by the sculptor Adamo Tadolini, the original lions are now in the Vatican Museums.

On the day of its inauguration, June 15, 1587, the fountain looked a little bare and the niches too empty in the eyes of the pontiff, who ordered a Moses worthy of Michelangelo from Giovanni Fontana. And so in 1589 a colossal statue of Moses, 4.27 meters high, was installed in the central niche. Executed by Leonardo Sormani with the collaboration of Prospero Antichi, the figure indicates the water flowing from the rock with its right hand and holds the Tables of the Law in its left. The episodes from the Bible represented in the bas-reliefs refer to Moses: *Aaron Leading the Israelites to Quench Their Thirst*, carved by Giovan Battista Della Porta and *Joshua Guiding the Soldiers and People of Israel to the Crossing of the Jordan*, by Flaminio Vacca and Pier Paolo Olivieri. The figure of Moses drew much criticism, some of it expressed in the so-called "pasquinades". But the most damning judgment is that of the art historian Adolfo Venturi, who described it as "disjointed, theatrical and clownish," and went on to call it "the vilest parody of Michelangeloism in Rome."

*Domenico
and Giovanni
Fontana,
Fountain of Moses
in Largo
San Bernardo,
1587-1589.*

Fountain of the Naiads

In the middle of the 19th century people began to look into the possibility of bringing the ancient Acqua Marcia back to Rome. For this purpose the Società dell'Acqua Pia Antica Marcia was set up and designed an aqueduct that took a shorter route than the original one and finished at Termini. Here, in the area between Via delle Terme di Diocleziano and Viale Einaudi, now occupied by gardens, the terminal fountain was built and inaugurated by Pius IX Mastai Ferretti (1846-1878) on September 11, 1870. Following the layout of Via Nazionale and the construction of two buildings by Gaetano Koch on the site of the old exedra of the baths, it was decided to move the fountain there, and its design was entrusted to Alessandro Guerrieri, chief engineer of the municipality.

Guerrieri created a modest fountain that was inaugurated in 1888 and temporarily decorated with four plaster lions. A commission was set up in 1897 to decide on the definitive decoration and, after examining various designs, entrusted the task to the Palermitan sculptor Mario Rutelli.

In 1901 Rutelli cast four groups of nymphs riding on sea monsters in bronze, to which he added the central group with Glaucus ten years later.

At the center of a round basin surrounded by a dense ring of jets stands the mighty statue of Glaucus, almost five meters tall, holding in his arms a dolphin from whose mouth spurts a powerful jet of water. Around the central basin are four smaller ones with platforms on which are set the four groups of the Naiads.

The colossal bronze groups, representing the nymph of

Gaetano Koch,
Piazza
della Repubblica,
1887-1898.

Alessandro
Guerrieri
and Mario Rutelli,
Fountain
of the Naiads

in Piazza della
Repubblica,
1888-1912,
whole
and details.

the seas with a horse, the nymph of the lakes with a swan, the nymph of the underground waters reclining on a monstrous reptile and the nymph of the rivers accompanied by a monster in the form of an eel, caused a sensation even before they were inaugurated. The nymphs were thought too provocative, with unseemly, indecent and immoral attitudes, by some councilors, even though they had been on the building commission that had approved Rutelli's designs. The fuss so stirred the curiosity of the Romans that they broke down the palings that still hid the fountain, resulting in its abrupt inauguration.

In the eyes of the public Rutelli's nymphs were not at all scandalous. On the contrary they were well received, and regarded as ennobling the modest fountain designed by Guerrieri.

*Alessandro
Guerrieri
and Mario Rutelli,
Fountain
of the Naiads
in Piazza
della Repubblica,
1888-1912,
detail.*

47

Piazza della Rotonda

The square is dominated by the Pantheon, the temple erected by Marcus Agrippa, prefect of the empire, in 27 BC on his return from the victorious campaign in Persia. It was rebuilt completely only a century later by Hadrian, although he did preserve the original inscription. In AD 608 the Byzantine emperor Phocas donated it to Pope Boniface IV (608-615), who turned it into a Christian church and renamed it Santa Maria ad Martyres at a ceremony of consecration held on May 13, 609. An extraordinary example of Roman architecture, the Pantheon has come down to us in an excellent state of preservation notwithstanding the despoliations to which it has been subjected over the centuries. The last of these took place in 1624, when Urban VIII Barberini (1623-1644) ordered the bronze facings to be stripped off the beams of the pronaos and melted down. Part of the enormous quantity of bronze obtained in this way was used by Bernini for the spiral columns of the baldachin in St. Peter's and the rest to cast a large number of cannons for Castel Sant'Angelo. So shocked were the Romans by this that they came up with a pasquinade which became a proverb: "Quod non fecerunt barbari fecerunt Barberini" (What the barbarians did not do the Barberini did). The temple, which once stood at the top of a flight of steps, is now at the same level as the square onto which the pronaos faces. Adorned with sixteen monolithic granite columns that are 13 meters high and

arranged to form a nave and two aisles, this porch provides access to the round cella roofed by a magnificent dome, a masterpiece of engineering, that has an oculus with a diameter of 9 meters at the center.

Fountain by Giacomo Della Porta

The fountain at the center of the square is the product of two interventions: the first by Pope Gregory XIII Boncompagni (1572-1585) and the second by Clement XI Albani (1700-1721), who also wanted to leave a memorial to himself in front of the monument sacred to paganism and to Christianity. The quatrefoil basin in African gray marble was designed by Giacomo Della Porta and made in 1575 by Leonardo Sormani, along with the baluster that supported the bowl, from which the water spouted. Set on a tiered platform of travertine, also Sormani's work, with five steps on the side of the Pantheon and only two on the other, owing to the sloping surface of the square, the basin is decorated with four groups of masks and dolphins attributed to Simone Moschino and originally intended for the Fountain of Neptune in Piazza Navona. In 1711 the fountain was altered by Clement XI, a collector and antiquarian under whose pontificate the city seethed with beautifications and reconstructions: the baluster with a bowl was replaced by rockwork decorated with dolphins and masks by Vincenzo Felici. On this was set the small Egyptian obelisk of Rameses II, 6 meters high, taken from Piazza di San Macuto.

Piazza della Rotonda, aerial view and Fountain of the Pantheon by Giacomo Della Porta and Leonardo Sormani, 1575, refashioned in 1711.

Fountain of the Pantheon, detail of the mask with dolphins by Simone Moschino, 1575, and, below, detail of the rockwork by Vincenzo Felici, 1711.

Pages 50-51, Vincenzo Felici, Fountain of the Pantheon, detail of the rockwork, 1711.

Piazza della Minerva

The small square is characterized by the charming monument at its center, known as the "pulcino della Minerva," a corrupted form of "Minerva's little pig," and set in front of the bare façade of the Church of Santa Maria sopra Minerva: a marble elephant covered with a precious caparison, sculpted in 1667 by Ercole Ferrata to a design by Gian Lorenzo Bernini, and supporting a small Egyptian obelisk from the 6th century BC, found two years earlier on the site of the Temple of Isis and Serapis, erected by Domitian and destroyed at the end of the 16th century.

The elephant was commissioned by Pope Alexander VII Chigi (1655-1667), who had an inscription in Latin car-ved on its base saying that a strong mind is needed to support a solid knowledge. On the east side of the square the Church of Santa Maria sopra Minerva was built in the 8th century over the ruins of the temple erected by Pompey in honor of the goddess. Collapsing five centuries later, it was rebuilt from 1280 onward and finished in the mid-15th century with the construction of the Renaissance façade. Divided in three by pilaster strips and crowned by a simple cornice, the plain front of the church has three portals, surmounted by three large circular *oculi*. The only decorations are the lunettes above the doors at the sides and the coats of arms of Francesco Orsini and Pius V Ghislieri (1566-1572) above the one in the middle.

*Piazza
della Minerva.*

Fountain of Via Santo Stefano del Cacco

Set up in the courtyard of Palazzo Altieri in the middle of the 17th century, the fountain was moved to the outside of the rear façade of the same building on Via Santo Stefano del Cacco in 1874. A plaque above the fountain, set in a simple architectural facing, records the date of the transfer and is surmounted by the Altieri coat of arms, with the six eight-pointed stars of Pope Clement X (1670-1676). The fountain consists of a marble sarcophagus from the Roman era, raised on two travertine supports, which collects the water flowing from two pipes set in the facing. The front of the sarcophagus is carved in bas-relief with two winged putti holding a shield adorned with the head of Medusa, flanked by two more putti. Below them are a bow, a quiver and two squirrels nibbling walnuts spilling out of two upturned vases.

Fountain of Via Santo Stefano del Cacco, 17th century.

Fountain of the Porter

Realized during the Renaissance, when work began on the repair of the Roman aqueducts, destroyed by barbarians in the Middle Ages, the Fountain of the Porter celebrates the trade of the water carrier, but it also commemorates the decline in the power of the guild of "water sellers" following the multiplication of fountains in squares and in the courtyards of Roman palaces.

Commissioned at the end of the 16th century to Jacopino del Conte, a Florentine painter resident in Rome, the small fountain was set in the façade of his home, Palazzo Grifoni on Via del Corso, opposite the Church of San Marcello. With the construction of Palazzo De Carolis on Via del Corso by Alessandro Specchi between 1714 and 1724, the small Palazzo Grifoni was incorporated into the new building and the fountain shifted a small distance, to a trabeated aedicule. In 1872 the fountain was moved again, as it was obstructing traffic, to its present location, set in the left side of the same Palazzo De Carolis, on Via Lata.

The fountain, fed by the Acqua Vergine, represents a water vendor with his barrel, from which the water flows into a small semicircular basin.

The Facchino (porter), along with the better-known Pasquino and Marforio, is a member of the "congress of the witty," i.e. a large group of "talking statues" used by the Romans to give ironic and somewhat malicious voice to the populace.

Piazza Sant'Ignazio

A singular example of late roman Baroque, the small square contrasts the Church of Sant'Ignazio with an array of small bourgeois townhouses, designed in 1726 by the Neapolitan architect Filippo Raguzzini (c. 1680-1771) as theatrical wings for the imposing façade of the Jesuit church, at the behest of Pope Benedict XIII Orsini (1724-1730).

Raguzzini reworked a theme already formulated by Borromini in the façade of the Church of San Carlo alle Quattro Fontane, but without any flair: moreover the daunting bulk of the Church of Sant'Ignazio, which houses the astonishing frescoes of Andrea Pozzo, the quintessence of illusory space, makes the square look irremediably cramped, and the scenic effect is not helped by the modest buildings that surround it. The townhouses, nicknamed "burrò" (*bureaux*) for their characteristic appearance, reminiscent of the furniture of the period, have a curvilinear form and simple façades, animated by the alternation of windows, balconies and balustrades.

Fountain of the Porter in Via Lata, 16th century.

Piazza Sant'Ignazio by Filippo Raguzzini, 1727.

Church of Sant'Ignazio, façade, begun in 1626.

55

Piazza Navona

Occupying the site of the stadium built by Domitian in the 1st century AD, the square has a regular shape, since the first houses built there in the 15th century stood on the ruined tiers of the circus. Its present appearance, which makes it the most beautiful Baroque square in Rome, is due to the interventions of Pope Innocent X Pamphilj (1644-1655), who was responsible for the construction of the Church of Sant'Agnese, begun by Girolamo and Carlo Rainaldi in 1652 and finished by Borromini in 1657, of Palazzo Pamphilj, on the left side of the church, erected by Girolamo Rainaldi between 1644 and 1650 and now the Brazilian Embassy,

and of the fountains. A place originally used to stage tournaments and horse races, the square, which had a concave bottom, used to be flooded in the month of August from the 17th century onward by closing the drainage channels of the fountains, and became a setting for princes and prelates to parade in their carriages. Today the concave façade of Borromini's church, flanked by two campaniles that serve to link the façade with the dome, forms, together with the sumptuous Pamphilj, Braschi, Lancellotti and other less well-known palaces, the backdrop to the spectacular scenery of the square, animated by the light that reflects off the water of the fountains.

Piazza Navona, panoramic view with the Fountain of the Moor and the Fountain of the Four Rivers.

Gian Lorenzo Bernini, Fountain of the Four Rivers, 1648-1651, detail.

INNOCENTIVS DECIMVS PON
NILOTICIS AENIGMATIBVS EXARATVM LAPIDEM
AMNIBVS SVBTERLABENTIBVS IMPOSVIT
VT SALVBREM
SPATIANTIBVS AMOENITATEM
SITIENTIBVS POTVM
MEDITANTIBVS ESCAM
MAGNIFICE LARGIRETVR

Fountain of the Four Rivers

One of the highest expressions of Bernini's talent, the Fountain of the Four Rivers is a work of architecture as well as sculpture: the handing of the fountain's disposition of masses reflects a subtle grasp of urbanistic factors, in which the image of water plays a far from minor role, becoming an architectural member in its own right.

At the center of a large basin stands a rocky base with four allegorical figures of rivers grouped around an obelisk: they are personifications of the Nile, with his face covered, as the source of the river was still unknown, the Ganges, the Danube and the Rio de la Plata, whose left hand is raised to protect himself from the possible collapse of the dome of the Church of Sant'Agnese, built by Bernini's rival Francesco Borromini. In representing the parts of the known world by the four rivers, surmounted by the pontifical coat of arms, Innocent X's aim was to assert the supremacy of the papacy at a politically difficult moment, in which the Protestant countries had achieved greater influence with the Peace of Westphalia in 1648. The granite obelisk is a Roman copy from the time of Domitian, found broken into pieces in the Circus of Maxentius on the Via Appia, where it had been erected by the emperor in AD 309. The obelisk was transported to the square in 1648 and the following year was raised on top of the rockwork. Following the installation of the statues, designed by Bernini and carved by the sculptors Antonio Fancelli, Claude Poussin, Antonio Raggi and Francesco Baratta, the fountain was unveiled on June 12, 1651.

Behind this evocative composition iconologists have discerned a cosmic symbolism, that stems from Bernini's frequentation of the Jesuit scholar Athanasius Kircher, a collector and Egyptologist held in high esteem by Pope Innocent X Pamphilj, who commissioned a study of the obelisk to him. Kircher assigned the obelisk an esoteric value, as a vehicle through which the divine essence passes into the four continents. Yet there are many cryptic symbols used by Bernini that find no explanation in the Jesuit's study, leaving the Fountain of the Four Rivers cloaked in a veil of mystery.

Gian Lorenzo Bernini, Fountain of the Four Rivers in Piazza Navona, 1648-1651, detail.

Southern Fountain: Fountain of the Moor
In front of Palazzo Pamphilj, constructed by Innocent X for his sister-in-law Olimpia Maidalchini, married to Prince Camillo Pamphilj, stands the Fountain of the Moor, a nickname that derives from the exotic features of the statue of the triton struggling with a dolphin, designed by Bernini and carved by Giovanni Antonio Mari in 1653. The fountain was originally composed of a multifoil basin in portasanta marble, made together with its twin of the Fountain of Neptune by Giacomo Della Porta in 1575 and decorated with four tritons spouting water from their double trumpets, which Della Porta had already designed for his fountain in Piazza del Popolo, alternating with four masks flanked by dolphins. The fountain was given its present appearance by Bernini, who finished the Fountain of the Four Rivers in 1652 and then set to work on the fountains that flanked it. He eliminated the beautiful travertine baluster, that echoed the mixtilinear motif of the basin and inserted the fountain in a low pool that repeated the same shape. Bernini designed the group of the triton at the center of the fountain, an example of virtuosity and rhetoric intended to satisfy the tastes of Innocent X: a muscular triton stands on top of a shell and twists his body in a spiral to hold a dolphin that is attempting to slip between his legs.

The tritons and masks that we see today are 19th-century copies made by the sculptor Luigi Amici, while Della Porta's original sculptures were moved to the gardens of Villa Borghese in 1874.

Northern Fountain: Fountain of Neptune
At the northern end of Piazza Navona, the Fountain of Neptune was made by Giacomo Della Porta along with its twin at the other end and subsequently transformed by Bernini, but met a different fate, as it was not decorated until the end of the 19th century. The four masks carved for this fountain in 1575 to Della Porta's design were inexplicably located on the fountain in Piazza del Pantheon and not even Bernini took the trouble to adorn it. Finally, in 1874, the municipality of Rome staged a competition for the work of decorating the fountain. The execution of the central group of Neptune was assigned to the sculptor Antonio Della Bitta and the eight groups at the sides to Gregorio Zappalà. Realized in 1878, the sculptures were conceived as companions to the groups on the Fountain of the Moor: the central one consists of Neptune standing on a rock and fighting a sea monster, while in the lateral groups two Naiads and two seahorses alternate with four putti in a verist style.

Giacomo Della Porta and Gian Lorenzo Bernini, Fountain of the Moor in Piazza Navona, 1575 and 1653, sculptures by Giovanni Antonio Mari, 1653.

Giacomo Della Porta and Gian Lorenzo Bernini, Fountain of Neptune in Piazza Navona, 1575 and 1653, sculptures by Antonio Della Bitta and Gregorio Zappalà, 1878, whole and detail.

Fountain of Piazzetta di San Simeone

Of the original fountain, erected in 1589 by Giacomo Della Porta in Piazza Montanara near the Theater of Marcellus, nothing remains following a series of modifications and changes of location. Della Porta's fountain was very straightforward, perhaps the artist's most modest creation, and realized at private expense by the sculptor Pietro Gucci: the water flowed from two pipes, set in a central pillar, into a single molded bowl. In 1696 the nearby Monastery of Sant'Ambrogio paid for the construction of an upper cup in exchange for a flow of one ounce of water. A bowl supported by a baluster was then added to the old basin. The baluster stood in turn on a cube decorated with four large masks from which water spurts. In the 18th century Della Porta's basin was replaced, as is clear from an engraving made by Vasi in 1757, and in 1829 the new one was replaced again, this time with a basin decorated with the crests of the city of Rome and raised on a base. The much altered fountain then embarked on a series of journeys, as Piazza Montanara was demolished in 1932 to make room for what is now Via del Teatro Marcello. Transferred temporarily to the Giardino degli Aranci on the Aventino, the fountain eventually found a permanent home in 1973, when it was erected in front of Palazzo Lancellotti in Piazzetta di San Simeone. The building, commenced by Francesco da Volterra at the end of the 16th century and finished by Carlo Maderno the following century, has an elegant doorway at the front. Designed by Domenichino, it is framed by two columns and surmounted by a balcony.

Giacomo Della Porta and Pietro Gucci, Fountain of Piazzetta di San Simeone, 1589.

Piazza Sant'Eustachio

The square is named after the Church of Sant'Eustachio, founded in the 4th century AD by Emperor Constantine on the site of the saint's martyrdom, condemned to death along with his family for having refused to take part in a pagan rite. A general in Hadrian's army who lived in the 2nd century AD, Eustace had converted to Christianity after having a vision of a stag with a cross between its antlers while out hunting, a legend recounted on the trophy that crowns the church's façade. In 1831 the poet Gioacchino Belli devoted the amusing sonnet *Sant'Ustacchio* to the legend of St. Eustace, very dear to the people of Rome. In the small and irregular square the church, preceded by a portico with columns and flanked by a Romanesque campanile, stands between a Renaissance building designed by Giulio Romano that now houses offices of the Senate and a graceful townhouse with a façade frescoed with scenes from the life of St. Eustace by Federico Zuccari.

Fountain of the Books

The charming little Fountain of the Books, carved from travertine in 1926 to a design by Pietro Lombardi, is set against the Palazzo della Sapienza on Via degli Staderari. A niche contains four books with antique bindings, resting on two brackets symmetrically arranged on each side of a stag's head, symbol of the district. Water spurts from two pipes set in the spines of the books at the top and from two more camouflaged as bookmarks that stick out from the two volumes at the bottom.

*Piazza
Sant'Eustachio.*

*Pietro Lombardi,
Fountain
of the Books
in Via degli
Staderari, 1926.*

Piazza Sant'Andrea della Valle

Following the busy Corso Vittorio, you come to a square characterized by the Baroque façade of the Church of Sant'Andrea della Valle, famous as the setting for the first act of Puccini's *Tosca*. Begun in 1591 by Pier Paolo Olivieri, the construction of the church was entrusted in 1608 to Carlo Maderno, who built the splendid dome (1622-1625), the largest in Rome after that of St. Peter's. The façade designed by Carlo Rainaldi (1656-1665) is a sequence of Corinthian columns and architraved niches, where the alternation of solids and voids is underlined by the breaks in the trabeation and the tympanum. In front of the Church of Sant'Andrea della Valle stands a fountain designed by Carlo Maderno, built in 1616 for the now vanished Piazza Scossacavalli. Following the opening of Via della Conciliazione in 1937 the square was demolished and the fountain removed. After spending twenty years in storage, the fountain was reconstructed in Piazza Sant'Andrea della Valle, where it can be seen today.

Following the customary model, the fountain is composed of a mixtilinear basin and a baluster that supports the upper bowl, while a pool at the bottom surrounds the basin. The old bowl was lost in the transfer and has been replaced by a modern copy in concrete. The shaft is decorated with the dragon and eagle symbols of the Borghese family in reference to Pope Paul V Borghese (1605-1621) for whom it was made. The water spills out of the upper bowl and falls in a curtain into the basin underneath, in which four jets spout from the surface at the sides.

*Church
of Sant'Andrea
della Valle
in the square
of the same name,*

*façade by Carlo
Rainaldi,
1656-1665.*

*Carlo Maderno,
Fountain
in Piazza
Sant'Andrea
della Valle, 1616.*

Tureen Fountain

Now situated in front of the Church of Santa Maria in Vallicella, in Piazza della Chiesa Nuova, the Tureen Fountain was in fact designed for Campo de' Fiori by Giacomo Della Porta to a commission from Pope Gregory XIII Boncompagni (1572-1585). Erected at the center of the square, the fountain was composed of an elegant oval basin adorned with four bronze dolphins taken from the Fountain of the Turtles, from which the water flowed into a larger basin sunk in the ground and paved with travertine. The last fountain supplied by the Acqua Vergine, the Tureen Fountain, had to be located below the level of the road owing to the low pressure of the water, a stratagem that was to be used again by Pietro Bernini for the Fountain of the Barcaccia. The name "tureen" derives from the bell-shaped travertine cover placed on the fountain in 1622 on the orders of Pope Gregory XV Ludovisi (1621-1623) to avoid the abuse and neglect to which it had been subjected. With the addition of the lid the four dolphins were removed and have subsequently vanished, and the water was made to flow out of four rosettes symmetrically arranged on the sides of the basin. Following the alteration the Tureen Fountain remained in Campo de' Fiori until 1889, when it was removed to make way for the monument to Giordano Bruno. Preserved in the municipal storehouses, it was salvaged in 1924 and located in Piazza della Chiesa Nuova.

Piazza della Chiesa Nuova.

Giacomo Della Porta, Tureen Fountain in Piazza della Chiesa Nuova, c. 1581.

Campo de' Fiori

The name "Field of Flowers" recalls the open spaces, free of constructions, still to be found in Medieval Rome, but which vanished following the drawing up of the first plan for the development of the city under Pope Sixtus V (1585-1590). The return of the papal court to Rome with Eugenius IV (1431-1447) had already resulted in the emergence of new districts in the area that extends from Ponte Sisto to Ponte Rotto. Thus Campo de' Fiori became the main square, center of commercial activity, but also of city life, and the place where papal bulls and public notices were posted. At the center of the square stood the gallows, whose presence is recorded by the memorial to the philosopher Giordano Bruno, here executed for heresy on February 17, 1600. The work of Ettore Ferrari and unveiled on June 8, 1889, the somber bronze statue of Giordano Bruno is set on top of a tall base, decorated with reliefs depicting scenes from the philosopher's life. The square, which has housed an open-air market since 1869, is still one of the liveliest spots in the city, drawing locals as well as tourists in search of souvenirs. In fact Campo de' Fiori retains the color and vivacity, for which it has long been famous. The fountain in the square is a copy of the Tureen Fountain, removed in 1889 to make room for the monument to Giordano Bruno and reconstructed in Piazza della Chiesa Nuova in 1924.

Piazza Campo de' Fiori and the fountain, copy of the Tureen Fountain in Piazza della Chiesa Nuova, 1924.

Fountain of the Mask

On Via Giulia, the elegant street laid out on the orders of Pope Julius II Della Rovere (1503-1513), not very far from Piazza Farnese, stands the Fountain of the Mask, named after the large marble mask from the ancient Roman era inserted in its front. The fountain, now set against a 19th-century wall, originally stood at the center of a small square, as can be seen in a fine engraving made by the architect Alessandro Specchi in 1699. Constructed by the Farnese family and fed by the Acqua Paola from 1626 on, it is certainly contemporary with the twin fountains in Piazza Farnese. It has a rectangular granite basin of the Roman era, above which stands a marble façade with a volute on each side surmounted by the Farnese lily, originally carved from travertine but replaced in the 19th century by a copy in wrought iron.

The water spouts from the mask's half-open mouth and falls into a small semicircular bowl, from where it spills over into the granite basin underneath and then into the pond at street level. Tradition has it that on special occasions the fountain was supplied by the Farnese with wine instead of water, as happened on the third day after Pentecost in 1720 to celebrate the appointment of the nobleman Marco Antonio Zondadari as Grand Master of the Order of Malta.

Fountain of the Mask in Via Giulia, c. 1626.

Piazza Farnese

Jewel of Renaissance Rome, Piazza Farnese owes its beauty and its fame to Palazzo Farnese, an immense building that stretches all the way from the square onto which the main front faces as far as Via Giulia, and then through the arch of the Passetto Farnese to the Tiber. On the opposite bank stands the Villa Farnesina, built by Agostino Chigi between 1506 and 1520 and acquired by the Farnese in 1590. Commissioned by Cardinal Alessandro Farnese, the future Pope Paul III (1534-1549), the palace was begun in 1517 by Antonio Sangallo, who constructed the façade on the square, continued by Michelangelo in 1549 with the cornice and the central balcony and finished by Giacomo Della Porta in 1589. The façade is split into three orders by moldings decorated with the Farnese lilies: on the ground floor the arched and rusticated doorway is set in the middle of twelve architraved openings, replicated on the second floor by the same number of windows with embedded columns and gables, alternatively round and triangular in shape, which frame Michelangelo's architraved loggia with double columns, surmounted by the Farnese coat of arms. Finally, the third floor has thirteen simpler windows with triangular gables, topped by Michelangelo's majestic cornice.

Antonio da Sangallo, Michelangelo, Giacomo Della Porta,

Palazzo Farnese in the square of the same name, 1517-1589.

The Fountains of Piazza Farnese

The fountains on two sides of the square are made from two basins of gray granite from the Baths of Caracalla, that were placed in Piazza Venezia in 1466 by Paul II Barbo (1464-1471) and arranged at an angle to the façade of the Renaissance Palazzo Venezia. At the behest of Paul III Farnese (1534-1549), one of the basins was moved to the center of Piazza Farnese to be turned into a fountain, but owing to the lack of water the basin served a solely ornamental purpose. Later, Gregory XIII Boncompagni (1572-1585) conceded the use of the second basin to the Farnese family, who transferred it to Piazza Farnese in 1580. But the flow of the Acqua Vergine that reached the square was not sufficient to supply the two fountains, which had to wait for the Acqua Paola, conceded to the Farnese by Gregory XV Ludovisi (1621-1623), to be activated. Finally, in 1626, the magnificent basins decorated with lion's heads were turned into fountains by Girolamo Rainaldi, who set them on top of two larger travertine basins of elongated shape and placed a baluster at the center of each, supporting a quatrefoil bowl with the Farnese lily in the middle.

Girolamo Rainaldi, fountain in Piazza Farnese, 1626.

Fountain of the Monte di Pietà

Backing onto the Palazzo del Monte di Pietà, the fountain was built at the beginning of the 17th century on the orders of Pope Paul V Borghese (1605-1621). The composition is an original and interesting one, but the workmanship is crude: a mask flanked by two small dragons and surmounted by an eagle, both heraldic symbols of the Borghese family, is set on top of a simple basin with a rounded edge. The water spurts in a fan from the mouth of the mask and in a jet from the heads of the dragons, falling into the basin underneath.

Fountain of Piazza Cairoli

Built at the end of the 19th century, the fountain is made up of a large, square granite basin. At the center a granite pillar supports an ancient bowl, found in Piazza Cenci in 1877, during the clearance of the Ghetto. On the bowl in the middle stands another pillar that supports the second, smaller bowl, from which rises a jet of water that falls into the two basins below. The fountain, unveiled in 1890, is by the French architect Edouard André, who also laid out the little garden in the piazza to a commission from Baron Guglielmo Huffer.

Fountain of the Monte di Pietà in the square of the same name, early 17th century.

Edouard André, Fountain of Piazza Cairoli, 1890.

Piazza Campitelli

The long and narrow square is closed to the northeast by two large buildings set side by side, Giacomo Della Porta's Palazzo Capizucchi and Palazzo Spinola, formerly Albertoni, begun by Della Porta and finished by Girolamo Rainaldi. On the opposite side of the square stands the Church of Santa Maria in Campitelli, rebuilt between 1662 and 1667 by Carlo Rainaldi to house the miraculous image of the Virgin of Santa Maria in Portico, which was credited with having freed the city of plague in 1656. A late Baroque masterpiece, the church has a travertine façade of superimposed aedicules, unadorned with sculptures but enlivened by the dynamic play of the structural elements, which create intensely dramatic effects of light and shade.

Originally at the center of the square, the small fountain was constructed by Giacomo Della Porta in 1589 at a cost of three hundred scudi, met in part by the owners of the houses facing onto the square, such as the noble Capizucchi and Albertoni families, and the rest by the municipality, which also undertook to bring the Acqua Felice there. The fountain is composed of a mixtilinear travertine basin standing on a base of the same shape that serves to collect the water; above the basin, which is decorated with two masks with donkey's ears, the insignia of the Senate and the Roman People and the crests of the families, that had financed its construction, a chalice-shaped marble baluster, adorned with festoons, supports a bowl from which a jet of water

spurts. A century later, with the enlargement of the church by Rainaldi, the fountain proved to be located too close to the new building, disturbing the peace of the religious services to such an extent that Innocent XI Odescalchi (1676-1689), at the prompting of the friars of Santa Maria in Portico, decided in 1679 to move it to the opposite side of the square, where it now stands.

Piazza Campitelli and the fountain by Giacomo Della Porta, 1589.

Fountain of the Turtles

The Fountain of the Turtles, originally intended for Piazza Giudia, was then granted by the "Congregatione sopra le fonti," the commission of cardinals in charge of public fountains, to the nobleman Muzio Mattei, along with a certain amount of water from the Acqua Vergine, in exchange for a commitment to meet the expense of its construction and maintenance and of paving the square. Appointed "architect of the fountains of Rome" by the Congregatione, Giacomo Della Porta built the fountain in the square in front of Palazzo Mattei between 1581 and 1584, in collaboration with the Florentine sculptor Taddeo Landini: abandoning his usual models, Della Porta created one of the most elegant fountains in Rome, in which the sculptural part prevails over the architectural one in the Florentine manner.

The model was undoubtedly the Fountain of Neptune in Piazza della Signoria in Florence, built by Bartolomeo Ammannati between 1563 and 1575, where the outside of the basin is decorated with pairs of satyrs and fauns in bronze.

At the heart of Della Porta's fountain are the four bronze youths straddling dolphins, sculpted by Taddeo Landini, which connect the shell-shaped basins of portasanta marble with the upper bowl of African gray marble, from which the water spurts through four small heads of putti. The turtles on the lip of the bowl were added by Bernini in 1658, on the occasion of its restoration at the behest of Alexander VII Chigi (1655-1667), when the steps that surrounded the fountain were eliminated because of the raising of the level of the square, and the pool was enlarged.

*Giacomo
Della Porta and
Taddeo Landini,
Fountain
of the Turtles
in Piazza Mattei,
1581-1584.*

Fountain of Piazza delle Cinque Scole

Originally located in the now vanished Piazza Giudia, in the middle of the ghetto, its place now occupied by Via del Portico di Ottavia, the fountain was made in 1591 by the sculptor Pietro Gucci to the design of Giacomo Della Porta. The material came from the large bases of columns in the so-called Tomb of Nero on the Pincio Hill. The fountain has a mixtilinear base of two steps on which rests a basin of more or less the same shape, made up of a sequence of arcs and semicircles. At the center of the basin a baluster supports a wide bowl, decorated on the outside with four masks, from which water spurts through the gaping and grimacing mouth. Snakes are woven into their long locks of hair, a motif inspired by the Gorgon.

The clearance of the ghetto at the end of the 19th century entailed the demolition of Piazza Giudia and the fountain, which was placed in the municipal storehouses. In 1924 the baluster and bowl were reutilized for a new fountain on the Gianicolo, near the Church of Sant'Onofrio, where they remained for a few years until the fountain of Piazza Giudia was reconstructed in Piazza delle Cinque Scole in 1930, close to its original location.

*Giacomo
Della Porta
and Pietro Gucci,
Fountain of Piazza
delle Cinque Scole,
1591.*

Piazza della Bocca della Verità

In the area of the Forum Boarium, the ancient cattle market, a huge square extends between the Palatino Hill and the Tiber. It is one of the most evocative places in the city, owing to the presence of monuments from different ages: Roman temples from the 2nd century BC, the Medieval Church of Santa Maria in Cosmedin and the Baroque Fountain of the Tritons. The two temples are known as the Temple of Vesta and the Temple of Fortuna Virilis, but have now been identified as the Temple of Hercules Victor and the Temple of Portunus, the god of ports. The Temple of Vesta is made up of a cylindrical cella built of blocks of marble ringed by twenty Corinthian columns, one of which has been lost along with the trabeation and roof. Both were converted into churches during the Middle Ages, dedicated to St. Stephen and St. Mary of Egypt respectively, and are in an excellent state of preservation, but are disused and can only be visited with permission from the Monuments and Cultural Heritage Service. Founded in the 6th century on the site of the *Ara Maxima Herculis* as a *diaconia*, i.e. a charitable institution, the Church of Santa Maria in Cosmedin was enlarged in 782 by Hadrian I and adorned with splendid decorations. These are the origins of the term "in Cosmedin," a corruption of the Greek word *kosmidion*, or ornament. Between 1715 and 1719, with the construction of the fountain, the church's Romanesque façade was decorated by Giuseppe Sardi to bring it into line with the prevailing Baroque taste. At the end of the 19th century the church was stripped of its 18th-century additions and returned to the simplicity of its Romanesque style, of which the campanile with seven stories of two- and three-light windows is a splendid example.

In the portico of the Church of Santa Maria in Cosmedin is the famous mask that has given the square its name: the *Bocca della Verità* is a large circular stone, originally a drain cover from the 3rd century AD, with a diameter of 1.75 meters, on which is carved the head of a faun with an open mouth. A legend embroidered by popular imagination holds that anyone who told a lie with his hand inserted in the mouth would have it bitten off.

Fountain of the Tritons

The Fountain of the Tritons was built in 1717 by the architect Carlo Bizzaccheri as part of the work on the layout of the square in front of the Basilica of Santa Maria in Cosmedin that had been ordered by Pope Clement XII Albani (1700-1721). In homage to the pontiff, Bizzaccheri designed an octagonal bowl with eight concave sides, forming an eight-pointed star, the heraldic symbol of the Albani family. The same motif is repeated in the step of the base, inscribed in a circular platform surrounded by sixteen low pillars linked by iron railings. Originally the enclosure had four openings providing access to the fountain at the points where four masks were set on the edge of the bowl, but these were removed at the end of the 19th century. In the middle of the basin is set a group of rocks carved out of travertine and decorated with water plants by Filippo Bai, on which kneel two powerfully built tritons, sculpted by Francesco Moratti, supporting a large scallop shell with their raised arms. In this fountain the influence of Bernini is evident, in both the rockwork and the tritons, but the eight-pointed basin, which gives an artistic unity to the whole, is a brilliant idea on Bizzaccheri's part. When the Acqua Felice was extended from the Campidoglio to Piazza della Bocca della Verità, the fountain was supplied with a flow of eight ounces of water, now reduced to two, that spurts above the shell from the three mountains topped with Clement XII's heraldic device, the eight-pointed star.

Carlo Bizzaccheri, Fountain of the Tritons in Piazza della Bocca della Verità, 1717.

Drinking trough on Lungotevere Aventino

At the same time as he created the Fountain of the Tritons, in 1717, Bizzaccheri built a drinking trough nearby: fountains built by the aristocracy were almost always accompanied by drinking places for animals. Bizzaccheri's *fontanile*, as such troughs are called, is the only one in the center of Rome and consists of a simple rectangular basin with rounded corners. The water flows into it from a lion's head located at one end. After 1870, with the construction of the embankments of the Tiber, the drinking trough was moved about a hundred meters onto the Lungotevere Aventino, where it can be seen today.

Carlo Bizzaccheri, drinking trough on the Lungotevere Aventino, 1717.

Fountain of the Mask of Santa Sabina

The Fountain of the Mask of Santa Sabina was created by Antonio Muñoz in 1936, using a mask from one of Giacomo Della Porta's fountains, taken from the municipal storehouses along with a granite basin from an ancient Roman bathhouse. The mask, framed in the valve of a shell, had been carved in 1593 by the stonecutter Bartolomeo Bassi for the fountain in Campo Vaccino: set against a large aedicule designed by Della Porta, the mask spouted water into a large granite basin found near the arch of Septimius Severus that was used as a drinking trough for the cattle that grazed freely in the Roman Forum. In 1818 Pope Pius VII Chiaramonti (1800-1823) had the basin transferred from Campo Vaccino to the foot of the obelisk in Piazza del Quirinale, while the mask was placed above a sarcophagus on the bank of the Tiber, opposite the Church of San Giovanni dei Fiorentini. From here it was moved again, following the construction of the Lungotevere Gianicolense, and then ended up in storage. With the transformation of the fortress of the Savelli, erected by Alberico II in the 10th century into Parco Savello, better known as "Parco degli Aranci" (Park of the Oranges), Muñoz was entrusted with the construction of the fountain in Piazza Pietro d'Illiria, created in 1614 by making a breach in the wall of the fortress. In the high brick wall that encloses the park, between the 15th-century portico with three arches of Santa Sabina on one side and the entrance to Parco Savello on the other, Muñoz created a niche in which to set the mask, from which water flows into the basin underneath.

Antonio Muñoz, Fountain of the Mask of Santa Sabina in Piazza Pietro d'Illiria, 1936.

Fountain of Sant'Alessio

The fountain comes from the courtyard of Palazzo Ac-coramboni in Piazza Rusticucci, destroyed with the opening of Via della Conciliazione. Although the square and palace were demolished, the small Baroque fountain was preserved and reconstructed in 1937 on the right-hand side of the Church of Sant'Alessio, on Via di Santa Sabina. Against a backdrop of rockwork, carved from small blocks of limestone, emerge the head and wings of a putto from which water flows into a small oval basin, supported by an eagle with open wings that in turn pours the water into a semicircular basin on the ground.

*Fountain
of Sant'Alessio
in the public
garden next
to the church
of the same name,
17th century.*

Fountain of the Amphorae

Constructed in 1927 for Piazza Testaccio and moved in 1935 to Piazza dell'Emporio, in front of the Ponte Sublicio, the Fountain of the Amphorae was the first in a series of public fountains in the old quarters of the city designed by Pietro Lombardi, architect of the Fascist regime, between 1926 and 1927.

The iconography of the fountain alludes to the legend of Monte Testaccio, formed of fragments of amphorae left over from the commercial activity of the ancient river Port of Ripa Grande, destroyed at the end of the 19th century with the construction of retaining walls along the Tiber.

The fountain has a circular plan subdivided into four segments, each with a flight of five concentric steps and a small basin at the top into which the water falls from pipes set in the base of the central structure. This is made up of a group of amphorae that are linked by brackets and volutes to the monumental base, surrounded by twelve low columns arranged on two levels. At each of the four ends of the base is set an amphora from which water flows out of a simulated crack.

Pietro Lombardi,
Fountain
of the Amphorae
in Piazza
dell'Emporio,
1927.

Fountain of Piazza d'Aracoeli

At the foot of the flight of steps leading up to the Campidoglio, before you get to Piazza Venezia, stands a small fountain designed by Giacomo Della Porta and executed in 1589 by the stonecutters Pietro Gucci, Andrea Brasca and Pace Naldini. Della Porta designed a mixtilinear basin, set on a base with two steps that repeats its undulating lines and surrounded by a channel to collect the water that flows from four lion's heads at the sides of the basin. Above the basin rises a baluster with a square base decorated with festoons and masks that supports the bowl with four putti pouring water from small amphorae. At the beginning of the 18th century, during the pontificate of Clement XI Albani (1700-1721), the base with its two steps and surrounding channel was replaced by a circular pool, ringed by a balustrade interspersed with low columns.

Giacomo Della Porta, Fountain of Piazza d'Aracoeli, 1589.

Santa Maria in Aracoeli and Campidoglio, panoramic view.

Pages 84-85, Giacomo Della Porta, Fountains of the Lions on the Campidoglio ramp, 1582-1588.

Campidoglio

The center of power in ancient Rome, seat of the Senate and site of the Temple of Jupiter, the Campidoglio, or Capitol, is still the home of the City Council, which meets in the main hall of the Palazzo Senatorio. In the Middle Ages the area gradually fell into decay, as a result of barbarian raids and the conflict between the Commune and the Church in the control of the city. The 16th century saw a revival in the fortunes of the acropolis, thanks to Paul III Farnese (1534-1549), who decided to assemble the remains of ancient Roman civilization in the Piazza del Campidoglio, in celebration of the power of the past that was now in the hands of the papacy. Following the difficulties encountered during the visit of Emperor Charles V in 1536, Paul III decided to reorganize the Capitoline Hill, making it easier to ascend. Moving the access to the west side of the hill, the pope asked Michelangelo to repave the Piazza del Campidoglio and renovate the façades of the Palazzo dei Conservatori and Palazzo Senatorio. Michelangelo designed a square in the form of a trapezium, with the addition of a third building, the Palazzo Nuovo, in a symmetrical position. Work commenced in 1537 with the construction of the base for the equestrian statue of Marcus Aurelius, previously located in Piazza San Giovanni in Laterano, where for centuries it had suffered from damage and looting as it was believed to be a statue of Constantine. The bronze figure was initially erected alongside the existing Palazzo dei Conservatori, but between 1544 and 1547 it was moved to the center of the square, to the apex on which the ellipse outlined in the paving converged. The star inscribed in an oval now set in the pavement at this point is the work of the architect Antonio Muñoz, executed in 1940 on the basis of a 1567 engraving. In 1544 Michelangelo set about the construction of the monumental *Cordonata*, or ramped stair: broad and easy to climb, it is lined with balustrades that are made up of a series of ten columns for each step. In line with the center of the *Cordonata* is the double staircase of the Palazzo Senatorio, built by Michelangelo along with the central niche, terminal point of the perspective construction, to house the great ancient statue of Athena, formerly in the courtyard of the old Palazzo dei Conservatori. The statue that Michelangelo wanted was not placed in the niche until 1583 and ten years later, in 1593, replaced with a small and incongruous statue of Minerva seated, in porphyry and marble, that had been restored and transformed into the goddess Roma. Minerva, holding a spear in her left hand and a sphere in her right, was flanked by two stucco figures of barbarians, removed in the 18th century, in line with the iconography of *Roma Triumphans*. At the sides of the niche, set against the walls of the flights of steps, are two colossal travertine statues from the 1st century AD representing the Nile and the Tigris. Originally in Constantine's Baths on the

Quirinale, they had been transferred to the portico in front of the old Palazzo dei Conservatori at the beginning of the 16th century. The Tigris was turned into the Tiber by replacing the tiger with a she-wolf and adding the figures of Romulus and Remus. When Michelangelo died in 1564, the square was not yet finished, but the three buildings were completed the following century on the basis of his designs: while the Palazzo Senatorio differs considerably from the artist's conception, the Palazzo dei Conservatori and the Palazzo Nuovo, constructed in the second half of the 16th century, retain the mark of Michelangelo despite the changes made over the course of the work. Finally, the three buildings were rendered uniform by the addition a heavy cornice on top, surmounted by balustrades with statues. In 1582, two Egyptian lions carved from gray granite with pink veins, uncovered near the Church of Santo Stefano del Cacco, were located at the base of the *Cordonata*. Turned into fountains six years later, under the guidance of Giacomo Della Porta,

each of the lions was bored and fitted with a pipe in its mouth, from which the water flows into a travertine vase, and then into two basins underneath. On special occasions in the 17th century, the lions, along with other Roman fountains, flowed with wine, one with white and the other with red: an event that was greeted with enthusiasm by the city's population, which flocked to them with flasks and jugs. In the same years classical statues of the Dioscuri, Castor and Pollux, flanked by their horses were erected on two tall bases at the top of the *Cordonata*. These were Roman copies of Greek sculptures that had been found in the area of Monte Cenci, where a temple dedicated to them used to stand. On the balustrade of the square, at the sides of the Dioscuri, are set the so-called "Trophies of Marius," from the reign of Domitian (AD 81-96), transferred here in 1590 from the nymphaeum of the Acqua Giulia on the Esquilino, and statues of Constantine and his son Constantius II, brought here from Constantine's Baths in 1653.

Michelangelo,
Piazza
del Campidoglio,
begun in 1537.

Equestrian statue
of Marcus
Aurelius
in Piazza del
Campidoglio, late
2nd century AD.

Fountain of the goddess Roma

In 1587 the Acqua Felice was brought to the Campidoglio, its conduits running from Piazza Madonna dei Monti through the Roman Forum: in a radical alteration of Michelangelo's design, Sixtus V Peretti (1585-1590) decided to create a fountain under the staircase of the Palazzo Senatorio, in front of the niche with the goddess Roma. Following a probable refusal by Della Porta, a competition was held and the project was entrusted to Matteo Bartolani, who came up with a design for five large basins set one on top of the other in a cascade and surmounted by the group of the she-wolf with Romulus and Remus. Over the course of the work the design underwent significant modifications and the Fountain of the goddess Roma was unveiled with just the two lower basins, during the pontificate of Clement VIII Aldobrandini (1592-1605).

Marforio Fountain

The principal interlocutor of Pasquino, Marforio is numbered among the talking statues of the popular "Congress of the Witty." Found in the Roman Forum, in the vicinity of the Arch of Septimius Severus, the gigantic reclining statue, datable to the 1st century AD, represents a river god, or perhaps the Sea, as suggested by the didactic epigraph "Mare in Foro" under the statue, later corrupted into Marforio. In 1588 the statue of Marforio was transferred to Piazza San Marco and placed alongside an ancient porphyry basin, but the same year the statue was moved again and transported to the Campidoglio until a place could be found for it. In 1594 Giacomo Della Porta set it against the wall that bounds the Piazza del Campidoglio on the north side, where the Palazzo Nuovo would be built, inside a niche and underneath the colossal head of Constantine (now in the courtyard of the Palazzo dei Conservatori): converted into a fountain, the statue was restored by Ruggero Bescapè, who replaced the missing parts—the right foot, both the hands that now clasp two shells and part of the face—while Della Porta added a sea monster with two thick tails to the rocky base, from whose hideous head the water flows into a basin beneath. With the construction of the Palazzo Nuovo, around the middle of the 17th century, the Fountain of Marforio was dismembered and then reassembled in 1679 in the courtyard of the Palazzo dei Conservatori, now the seat of the Musei Capitolini. Finally, in 1734, a bust of Clement XII Corsini (1730-1740), responsible for some of the alterations made to the fountain, was set on top of a bracket at the front.

Matteo Bartolani, Fountain of the goddess Roma in Piazza del Campidoglio, 1588.

Giacomo Della Porta, Marforio Fountain in the courtyard of Palazzo Nuovo, 1594.

Piazza Venezia

Piazza Venezia was the first major urbanistic intervention in Renaissance Rome, carried out by Pope Paul II Barbo (1464-1471) around his own residence of Palazzo Venezia, constructed next to the Basilica of San Marco from 1455 onward, when he was still a cardinal. Enlarged over the following years, the palace became a vast architectural complex, comprising the Medieval Tower of the Biscia, raised and adorned with battlements, the papal palace and a *viridarium*. Built according to the Renaissance principles devised by Leon Battista Alberti, the papal palace is a rectangular block with towers at the corners and a porticoed courtyard in the middle. The façade is based on a system of carefully calculated relationships with the plan of the building and the dimensions of the square. The *viridarium* was originally a garden surrounded by a portico with an open gallery on top, until Paul III Farnese (1534-1549) walled up many of the arches in 1537, radically altering the significance of the original architecture of the building, which came to be known as "Palazzetto Venezia." In 1564 the complex was ceded

by Pius IV de' Medici (1560-1565) to the Republic of Venice as a seat for its ambassadors. Passing to France in 1797 and to Austria in 1814, it was confiscated by the Italian government in 1916 and, after a long restoration, converted into the seat of a museum and a number of cultural institutions. The palace currently houses the Museo di Palazzo Venezia, the Soprintendenza ai Beni Artistici and the library of the Istituto Nazionale di Archeologia e Storia dell'Arte. As part of the reorganization of Rome following its selection as capital in 1870, the monument to Victor Emmanuel II was built by Giuseppe Sacconi from 1885 onward. The construction of the *Altare della Patria* (Altar of the Fatherland), as the monument is known, to serve as a spectacular backdrop to Via del Corso, which formed the entrance to the city from the north, entailed an enlargement of the square. This required the demolition of a dense neighborhood of houses dating from the Middle Ages, the displacement of Palazzetto Venezia, reconstructed further back, and the construction of a building in a position symmetrical to Palazzo Venezia, the new offices of the Assicurazioni Generali, inaugurated in 1907.

On Sacconi's death in 1905, responsibility for the work was given to the architects Gaetano Koch, Pio Piacentini and Manfredo Manfredi, who in 1920, on the fiftieth anniversary of the unification of Italy, inaugurated the monument in the presence of Victor Emmanuel III. However, the decorative part, including Carlo Fontana's quadriga of Unity and Paolo Bartolini's quadriga of Liberty, was not completed until 1927.

While its structure recalls the elegant form of the Altar of Pergamum, the outsize monument is in fact a pompous creation, completely extraneous to the setting in which it is placed. The white marble building is characterized by a tall Corinthian colonnade set at the top of broad flights of steps. It is richly decorated with bronze statues, from the winged lions at the sides of the central flight of steps to the equestrian statue of Victor Emmanuel II at the summit of the same flight and the chariots drawn by four horses, with winged victories on the propylaea.

The *Altare della Patria* is an example of the *Umbertino* style, a current named after the reign of Umberto I that was typical of Roman architecture at the turn of the century, with its revival of Neorenaissance language in a decorative key. Set against the base of the *Altare della Patria* are two symmetrical fountains, composed of two simple semicircular basins that collect fans of water from two fissures in the marble. The basins are adorned with reclining statues representing the Adriatic and Tyrrhenian Seas, on top of pyramidal structures. The Adriatic, carved by Emilio Quadrelli in 1911, is a large recumbent figure whose head is covered by a shell and who appears to be shading his eyes from the light of the sun with his right hand, while the left hand caresses a lion, the symbol of Venice. Pietro Canonica's statue of the Tyrrhenian, executed the same year, is a reclining figure represented in the act of raising from a boulder, with the Capitoline she-wolf at his feet.

Giuseppe Sacconi,
Monument
to Victor
Emmanuel II
in Piazza Venezia,
begun in 1885,
detail.

Emilio Quadrelli,
Fountain of
the Adriatic Sea
in the monument
to Victor
Emmanuel II, 1911.

Pietro Canonica,
Fountain of
the Tyrrhenian Sea
in the monument
to Victor
Emmanuel II, 1911.

Piazza del Colosseo

The square is located in the valley bounded by the Palatino and Celio Hills and the Roman Forum and it is dominated by the Flavian Amphitheater, an enormous building known as the "Colosseum" in the Middle Ages, as it is the largest ancient Roman monument to have come down to us and thus is considered a symbol of the grandeur of Rome. Erected by Vespasian in the area which used to be occupied by the artificial lake in front of Nero's Domus Aurea, the Colosseum was inaugurated by Emperor Titus in AD 80 with games that lasted for a hundred days. The building, the first permanent Amphitheater in the city, contains an arena of elliptical shape with two monumental entrances at the ends of the main axis. The Amphitheater, clad entirely with slabs of travertine, could hold up to 50,000 spectators, seated on balconies that are subdivided into sectors along vertical axes, with the upper parts reserved for women. The external structure of travertine has three tiers of eighty arches each, framed by half-columns with Doric, Ionian and Corinthian capitals, concluded by an attic onto which were fixed the supports of the *velarium*, an immense awning used to shade the arena from the sun. Falling into disuse in the late Imperial age, it was turned into a fortress by the Frangipane family in the Middle Ages, before passing into the hands of the Senate in 1312, which used it as a stone quarry. After the building had been plundered for the construction of churches and palaces, including the Church of San Giovanni in Laterano, Palazzo Barberini and Palazzo Farnese, Pope Benedict XIV Lambertini (1740-1758) put an end to the barbarous despoliation in the 18th century, consecrating the arena to the Passion of Christ and having the fourteen stations of the *Via Crucis* built around it.

In 1808 the Colosseum was restored with the addition of a large buttress to consolidate the structure. However, the opening in 1933 of Via dell'Impero, now Via dei Fori Imperiali, has caused further deterioration with its intense traffic, a process that has only briefly been halted by a series of restorations, the most recent in 1992.

*Piazza
del Colosseo,
aerial view.*

*Colosseum,
80 AD.*

On the square, in the vicinity of Via di San Gregorio, stands another monument of the Roman world, the triumphal arch erected by the Senate to mark the tenth year (AD 315) of the reign of Emperor Constantine and commemorate his victory over Maxentius (AD 312). Built of Numidian marble and with three archways, it is partly decorated with reused material from older buildings, including reliefs from the time of Trajan and Marcus Aurelius and roundels that are probably from Hadrian's period. The Constantinian reliefs are characterized by a new vision that breaks with classical canons and favors instead a subordination of the subjects and a more rigid frontality, ushering in the late ancient period and foreshadowing Medieval art. At the intersection between Via Sacra and Via di San Gregorio, opposite the Arch of Constantine, are

the foundations of the Meta Sudans Fountain from the Flavian period (AD 80), whose remains were removed in 1936, following the implementation of Mussolini's city-planning scheme, as they were impeding the flow of traffic. The fountain's name derived from its conical shape, recalling the *metae* of the circus: water flowed down the 9-meter-tall shaft, emerging from a perforated sphere of bronze on the top. The excavations carried out in the area in the 1970s and 1980s proved fundamental in defining the contemporary method of archeological investigation.

*Arch of Constantine
in Piazza del
Colosseo, 315 AD,
whole and detail.*

Piazza Madonna dei Monti

At the heart of the popular Rione Monti, in the narrow Piazza Madonna dei Monti, Pope Sixtus V Peretti (1585-1590) commissioned to Giacomo Della Porta a fountain fed by the Acqua Felice that descended to the square from Piazza del Quirinale. The fountain is one of Della Porta's simplest and most elegant creations in the essentiality of its structure. Executed in 1588-1589 by the stonecutter Battista Rusconi, the fountain is composed of an octagonal base of four steps, surmounted by a travertine basin and adorned with two papal coats of arms and two municipal coats of arms. At the center of the basin stands a first baluster supporting a bowl, in which a second baluster holds a smaller bowl. The water emerges from a pipe in the upper bowl and then falls into the lower one, where it spurts through four lion's heads into the octagonal basin. On the square, around the fountain, stand the small Church of Santi Sergio and Bacco, an 18th-century townhouse, and the side of the beautiful Church of the Madonna dei Monti, built by Giacomo Della Porta in 1580 on the site where a miraculous image of the Virgin and Child had been found by chance the previous year. An interesting example of architecture from the period of transition between the Renaissance and the Baroque, the church has a dignified but austere façade, derived from that of the Church of the Gesù, a model that influenced religious architecture for almost a century.

Piazza Madonna dei Monti and the fountain by Giacomo Della Porta, 1588-1589.

Piazza Santa Maria Maggiore

The square gets its name from the majestic Basilica of Santa Maria Maggiore, founded in the 5th century to be the largest of all the churches dedicated to the Virgin and still outstanding in its grandeur and beauty. The product of interventions carried out in different periods, the basilica owes the harmonious cohesion of its various elements to Ferdinando Fuga: the spectacular façade, built by Fuga between 1741 and 1743, is set in front of the original one, preserving its mosaics, which can be seen through the arches of the loggia on top of the architraved portico. In the middle of the square stands a tall fluted column (14.30 meters high) with a Corinthian capital from the Basilica of Constantine, placed here in 1614 on the orders of Paul V Borghese (1605-1621) and topped by a bronze statue of the Virgin and Child, the work of the French sculptor Guillaume Berthelot. A year later, Paul V commissioned Carlo Maderno, architect of the *Reverenda Fabbrica di San Pietro*, who was already at work on the construction of the basilica's imposing façade, to build a fountain to replace the existing Medieval one at the foot of the column, consisting of a porphyry vase supported by columns. With the aid of the architect Gasparc De Vecchi, Maderno designed a large, mixtilinear oblong basin of travertine, set on a broad base of the same shape, in turn raised on four travertine steps. At the center of the basin a modest bowl stands on top of a simple baluster, a replacement

*Piazza
Santa Maria
Maggiore.*

for the original larger and richer one. On the long sides two eagles, the emblem of the Borghese family, spurt water into small semicircular basins, supported by volutes decorated with masks, while the two dragons, another Borghese emblem, at the ends of the short sides that used to pour water into the central basin were lost in the 19th century, when the level of the street was altered. On that occasion the fountain was rebuilt and the drinking trough set against the column on the opposite side to the fountain, also vanished.

Back to the basilica: its imposing rear part, characterized by the apse and the two domes and facing onto the Piazza dell'Esquilino, is the work of the architect Carlo Rainaldi (1669-1675), who set it at the top of a monumental flight of steps. At the center of the square stands an obelisk, found in the vicinity of the Mausoleum of Augustus and erected here by Sixtus V in 1587. The 14.80-meter-high obelisk is a Roman copy of Egyptian ones and used to flank the entrance of the mausoleum, along with the obelisk now in Piazza del Quirinale.

Piazza dell'Esquilino and the back part of the Basilica of Santa Maria Maggiore.

Carlo Maderno,
fountain
in Piazza
Santa Maria
Maggiore, 1615.

Piazza Vittorio Emanuele II

The square, in the middle of the Piedmontese quarter, is based on the English square model, with a central garden and monumental buildings for residential use at the sides. A fine example of city planning from the period of Umberto I, the square, surrounded by colonnades, is the largest in Rome: envisaged by the urban development scheme of 1873, it has been housing the city's biggest market since 1902. In 1911 a fountain with a circular basin and a sculptural group on top, made by Mario Rutelli, was placed in the gardens of the square. Originally conceived for the Fountain of the Naiads in Piazza della Repubblica, and immediately baptized "fritto misto" (mixed fish-fry) by the

Romans, the group consists of the interlaced figures of three tritons with a dolphin and a large octopus. In the gardens of the square, not far from Rutelli's statue, are the ruins of the nymphaeum of the Acqua Giulia, built by Emperor Severus Alexander in AD 226. Constructed of concrete faced with brick, the fountain was three stories high and culminated in a large central niche flanked by two arches, adorned with the so-called "Trophies of Marius," transferred in 1590 to the balustrade of the Campidoglio terrace. The fountain, which functioned as a water tower, served in the 16th century as a model for the terminal fountains of the aqueducts reconstructed by the popes, from Paul III to Sixtus V.

Piazza Vittorio Emanuele II and the fountain by Mario Rutelli, 1911.

Piazza San Giovanni in Laterano

One of the most celebrated squares in Christendom and the southern entrance to the city ringed by the Aurelian Walls, the area was first given a monumental appearance by Emperor Constantine, who in AD 321 donated the Lateran Palace, a huge and sumptuous building constructed by the wealthy clan of the Laterani in the 1st century AD, to the bishop of Rome, and built alongside it the ecclesia of San Giovanni in Laterano, along with the baptistery. The Lateran Palace, nicknamed the "Patriarchìo" because of its proximity to the patriarchal basilica, was the residence of the pope and the Curia until the 13th century. Over the seventy years in which the papacy was exiled to Avignon, the complex went through a period of decline. The return of the pontiff to Rome did not change things, since Gregory XI de Beaufort (1371-1378) made his residence in the Vatican, allowing the Lateran to fall into ruin. Left to its own devices, the complex was later chosen as the hub of an ambitious scheme of urban development by Sixtus V Peretti (1585-1590), which entrusted its implementation to his trusted architect Domenico Fontana. In his radical transformation of the square, Fontana demolished the old Patriarchìo, with the exception of the *Scala Santa* and the *Sancta Sanctorum*. Using the same layout as the Patriarchìo, Fontana constructed a new Lateran Palace on a square plan, taking his inspiration from Palazzo Farnese: the building has three identical faces, with three tiers of windows, whose tympana are alternatively curved and triangular and a central doorway surmounted by a balcony. Next to the Lateran Palace is the building of the *Scala Santa*, so-called because it contains what is held to be the staircase that Christ ascended to appear before Pilate and now leads to the ancient private chapel of the popes, the *Sancta Sanctorum*. The façade of the building, which has five arches, echoes that of the Loggia delle Benedizioni, also designed by Fontana, on the opposite side of the Lateran Palace, with its two tiers of five arches, surmounted by a pair of belfries dating from the 13th century. Following the construction of straight roads connecting the Lateran with Santa Maria Maggiore, the Colosseum and the Appia Antica, Fontana erected at the point where they come together an Egyptian obelisk in red granite, found broken into pieces near the Circus Maximus in 1587. The oldest and tallest in the city, the obelisk was brought to Rome in 357 by Constantius II, who had had it removed from the Temple of Ammon at Thebes, where it had been raised by the pharaoh Thutmose III in the 15th century BC.

Fountain of the Lateran Obelisk

At the foot of the obelisk is set a small fountain, built between 1603 and 1607 to a design commissioned to Domenico Fontana by the Lateran canons. Backing onto the obelisk, but originally separate from it, the fountain is composed of two dolphins that spout water into a ribbed marble basin, set on a base of three steps, and a front surmounted by a bronze statue of St. John the Evangelist reading between two Medici lilies, also in bronze. Decapitated by a bolt of lightning in the 19th century, the statue was removed for restoration, but all trace was lost of it along with the lilies. The front, flanked by two volutes, is decorated with the emblems of several popes, from Clement VIII Aldobrandini (1592-1605) to Paul V Borghese (1605-1621), to whom the eagle and two dragons carved in marble allude.

Piazza San Giovanni in Laterano.

Basilica of San Giovanni in Laterano in the square of the same name, 313-318 AD,

façade by Alessandro Galilei, 1732-1735, whole and detail.

Fountain of the Navicella

The unusual "Little Ship Fountain" was created in 1931 at the time of the layout of the square in front of the Church of Santa Maria in Domnica: at the center of a low oval basin a model of a Roman ship in marble, with a prow in the shape of a wild boar's head, stands on a marble base adorned with the emblems of Leo X de' Medici (1513-1521). Fed by the Acqua Felice, the vessel has a low jet of water rising from its central deck. The water then overflows from the deck at the sides and runs down the base into the large travertine basin.

The so-called "navicella," which had been placed in front of the church in 1518-1519 by Leo X, is generally considered to be a 16th-century copy of an ancient votive offering made to the goddess Isis, protectress of seafarers, by sailors of the fleet based at Cape Misenus who had survived a shipwreck. The existence of an older ship is confirmed by Pomponius Laetus, who in 1484 recorded its discovery in the vicinity of the Colosseum, on the site of the camp of the sailors of the Cape Misenus fleet, who were in charge of the complicated maneuvering of the great *velarium* of the Flavian Amphitheater.

Domenico Fontana, Fountain of the Lateran obelisk in Piazza San Giovanni in Laterano, 1603-1607.

Fountain of the Navicella in Via della Navicella, 1931.

Fountain of the Acqua Paola

On the top of the Gianicolo, a point which offers one of the most picturesque panoramas of the city, stands the imposing terminal Fountain of the Acqua Paola, erected by Flaminio Ponzio and Giovanni Fontana between 1610 and 1612. The Acqua Paola is named after Paul V Borghese (1605-1621), who in 1608 began to reactivate the aqueduct built by Trajan. Carried out under the supervision of Giovanni Fontana, this entailed repairing the ancient Roman conduits where possible and adding new ones along a route of 64 kilometers, bringing an abundant flow (about 1100 ounces) of extremely pure water into the city from the springs at Bracciano. However, the colossal undertaking, completed in less than two years, was not followed by the construction of fountains of any particular artistic significance, except for the large one on the Gianicolo, the Fountain of Ponte Sisto and one of the two fountains in St. Peter's Square. But numerous private fountains were built, as the capacious new aqueduct meant that water was no longer a privilege of the rich and became available to all, making its way into people's homes. Once the Acqua Paola had been brought to Rome, the pontiff commissioned to the same architects a terminal fountain on a scale that would reflect and be worthy of the enormous enterprise and the large quantity of water that it supplied. Giovanni Fontana designed a gigantic fountain inspired by that of the Acqua Felice, whose large dimensions are handled in a harmonious way: the water flows in abundance through three large niches, flanked by

two smaller ones and surmounted by an attic in which is set a large marble slab with a beautiful and solemn inscription celebrating Paul V. The attic is crowned in turn by the pope's coat of arms supported by two angels, carved by the sculptor Ippolito Buzio, while at the sides there are two eagles, heraldic devices of the Borghese family. Much of the material used in the construction of the fountain was marble from the demolished Temple of Minerva in Nerva's Forum; while the granite columns that flank the main arches at the front come from the old façade of the Constantinian St. Peter's Basilica. In 1690 the architect Carlo Fontana replaced the five small basins that collected the water with a large pool of white marble, that gives the fountain a more majestic appearance.

Flaminio Ponzio and Giovanni Fontana, Fountain of the Acqua Paola on the Gianicolo, 1610-1612.

Fountain of Ponte Sisto

Originally constructed in 1879 on the left bank of the Tiber, against the wall of the Ospizio dei Mendicanti at the beginning of the Via Giulia, the fountain was removed when work started on the embankments of the river. It was rebuilt twenty years later, in 1898, in Piazza Trilussa on the opposite bank of the Tiber. A memory of its original location survives in the inscription on the attic celebrating Paul V Borghese (1605-1621) for having brought water from the summit of the Gianicolo to the city on the eastern side of the Tiber. The fountain is now situated under the Gianicolo, in the Rione Trastevere, and this makes it possible to take in at one sweep the Fountain of Ponte Sisto and the terminal Fountain of the Acqua Paola in the backdrop, with which it presents close similarities. Constructed in 1613 by the Flemish architect Jan van Santen (known as Giovanni Vasanzio in Italy), with the collaboration of Giovanni Fontana, it consists of a large tunnel-vaulted niche flanked by two marble columns with Ionian capitals that support an architraved molding, on which the attic is set. The water, which once also gushed from a wide opening at the top into a small basin underneath and then flowed in a fan into the large basin at street level, now spurts from the mouths of the two dragons carved on the bases of the columns, in two powerful jets of water that intersect in the middle, while two lion's heads at the ends spray jets of water into the same basin.

*Piazza Trilussa
and the Fountain
of Ponte Sisto by
Jan van Santen,
1613.*

Fountain of Piazza Mastai

When the Neoclassical building of the Manifattura dei Tabacchi was constructed in 1863, Pope Pius IX Mastai Ferretti (1846-1878) commissioned to the architect Andrea Busiri Vici a monumental fountain for the square in front, stipulating that it should not block the view of the building's façade. In 1865 Busiri Vici created a modest but decorous fountain, based on the traditional module of the mixtilinear basin surmounted by two bowls. On an octagonal base with three steps is set a travertine basin of the same shape, at whose center a baluster of four dolphins with their tails interlaced stands on an octagonal base and supports a bowl. This in turn houses four putti surmounted by a second, upside-down bowl decorated with scales. The water emerges from a pipe in the upper bowl and then flows down into the second bowl, from which it spouts through four lion's heads into the basin underneath. The fountain has many points in common with the ones created by Della Porta in Piazza Madonna dei Monti, in terms of its overall design, and Piazza d'Aracoeli, for the baluster with putti, but above all it resembles the nearby Fountain of Santa Maria in Trastevere.

Andrea Busiri Vici, Fountain of Piazza Mastai, 1865.

Fountain of the Prigione

The Fountain of the Prigione (prisoner) comes from the now vanished Villa Peretti Montalto on the Esquilino, the beautiful residence built by Domenico Fontana in 1580 for Pope Sixtus V Peretti (1585-1590), and is the only one of the villa's fountains to have survived its demolition at the time of the construction of the Termini railroad station. Dismantled in 1877 and placed in the storehouses of the Ministero degli Interni, the fountain was reconstructed on the slopes of the Gianicolo in 1938, in a widening of Via Mameli that acts as a scenic backdrop to Via Luciano Manara. The fountain is composed of a niche decorated with festoons and lion's heads on the inside, framed by two pilasters that support the architrave surmounted by a pediment; two lavish volutes at the sides link the niche to the abruptly interrupted parapet. In the middle of the niche, where once stood the marble half-length figure of a prisoner, which gave the fountain its name but has now been lost, the water now spurts from a lion's head.

Domenico Fontana, Fountain of the Prigione in Via Mameli, c. 1580.

Fountain of Piazza Santa Maria in Trastevere

This is without question the oldest of the city's public fountains. In fact it appears on a plan of the city dating from 1472, alongside an inscription referring to the curious tradition of the Spring of Oil. This last derives from the pagan story of an eruption of oil at an unspecified location on the Tiber, identified from the 4th century AD onward as the Piazza di Santa Maria in Trastevere, where in the time of Augustus there had been a fountain called the *Fons oletus* as it was fed by water that was not safe to drink, a name that was rapidly corrupted into *Fons olei*. Frontinus, author in AD 97 of an important work on the city's waters and aqueducts, the *De aquaeductu urbis Romae*, speaks of public fountains built by Augustus and supplied by the Acqua Alsietina, water from an unwholesome source that the emperor had brought to Rome to fill the *naumachia*, a gigantic pool used to stage mock naval battles in the vicinity of what is now Piazza Santa Maria in Trastevere. The Acqua Alsietina fed the fountain in the square until 1590-1591, when it was replaced by the Acqua Felice, brought to Rome a few years earlier by Sixtus V Peretti (1585-1590), and then by the more plentiful Acqua Paola in 1659. The fountain depicted on the plan of 1472, built in the middle of the 15th century on the site of one from the Augustan age and consisting of a square basin raised on several steps and surmounted by two bowls, subsequently underwent numerous reconstructions and restorations, but without altering its original structure. The first documented reconstruction is recorded by

Vasari in his *Lives*, where it is attributed to Bramante, between 1496 and 1501, under the pontificate of Alexander VI Borgia (1492-1503). However, the most important restoration was the one carried out in 1659 by Gian Lorenzo Bernini on behalf of Alexander VII Chigi (1655-1667), who had the square paved and the fountain, which used to be located on the opposite side, moved to the center of the square, in front of the Basilica of Santa Maria Maggiore. When he restored the fountain, Bernini added four large shells facing into the basin, which collected the water from the bowl on top of the baluster and poured it into four shells set alongside the first but facing outward. In 1692 Pope Innocent XII Pignatelli commissioned a new restoration to Carlo Fontana, who replaced Bernini's shells with others of his own design, but still inspired by the same artist's Fountain of the Bees. Finally, in 1873, the municipality of Rome, as we are informed by the inscription on one side of the basin, decided to return the fountain "to its original design," reconstructing it in marble on the same model in travertine. The fountain is still located at the center of the square, where it is raised on an octagonal travertine base with seven steps. It consists of a square marble basin, with the corners cut off so that it looks octagonal, and has a baluster with a square base at the center that supports a marble bowl.

Piazza Santa Maria in Trastevere and the 15th-century fountain, restored by Bernini in 1659.

Piazza Giuseppe Gioacchino Belli

When crossing the river by Ponte Garibaldi, Piazza Belli constitutes the northern entrance to Trastevere, from the Latin *trans Tiberim*, i.e. across the Tiber, an area urbanized in the republican era and characterized by commercial facilities connected with the port on the opposite bank. In the 14th century, with the exile of the popes to Avignon, the suburb of Trastevere, which like the other areas across the Tiber had been under the pope's jurisdiction, came under the administration of the city, becoming the 13th *rione* (district) of Rome. Over the following centuries the urbanization of the area was completed, commencing with the construction of Ponte Sisto (1475) and the two parallel streets on the opposite banks of the river, Via della Lungara and Via Giulia, which established rapid communications between the Rione Trastevere, the Vatican and the city to the east of the river. In the 18th and 19th centuries important charitable institutions were created in the district, such as Filippo Raguzzini's Hospital of San Gal-

licano, a model for future hospital architecture, along with commercial structures like the Manifattura dei Tabacchi. The square, named after the great Roman dialectal poet Giuseppe Gioacchino Belli (1791-1863), is laid out around the Medieval Palazzetto Anguillara, which now stands in isolation along with its battlemented tower following the demolition of the surrounding urban fabric as a result of the opening of Viale Trastevere in 1888. In the middle of the square stands the monument to Belli, carved in 1913 by Michele Tripisciano, a Sicilian sculptor who refused payment for the work, commissioned to him by a citizens' committee.

A homage, as the inscription on the parapet tells us, paid by the Roman people to their poet, the monument presents Belli in a top hat and with a wooden stick, stolen several times and eventually replaced by an iron one, painted an ebony color. The poet stands on a tall plinth, adorned at the sides with twin fountains: set at the top of three steps, two trefoil marble basins receive the water from bearded masks at the center of volutes.

Piazza Giuseppe Gioacchino Belli and the monument to the poet by Michele Tripisciano, 1913.

St. Peter's Square

An extraordinary example of Baroque architecture, St. Peter's Square owes its glory to Gian Lorenzo Bernini, undisputed arbiter of the Roman artistic milieu from the third decade of the 17th century onward. He laid out an elliptical colonnade in the space in front of St. Peter's, divided into two hemicycles that radiate out from the façade of the basilica. Bernini created a spectacular setting, a symbol of the Church in the Baroque era: starting from the colonnade, whose open shape creates an urbanistic and symbolic link between the building and the city, the faithful are led into the basilica and conducted toward the high altar, emphasized by the baldachin, and finally to the throne of St. Peter, in the apse, the climax of an imaginary mystical-symbolic route. Bernini carried out his research on the borderline between sculpture and architecture, in pursuit of a powerful aspiration to overcome the hierarchies of their respective artistic languages and achieve a unity of representation. The end result obtained in St. Peter's Square is that of a well-proportioned and harmonious whole, a total work of art, a "theatrical production" rich in special effects. The square is located on the site of the ancient circus of Caligula, where Nero had a large number of Christian martyrs put to death around the middle of the 1st century AD. One of them was Peter, and in AD 320 Constantine began to build a Latin-cross basilica with a nave and four aisles over his tomb. Completed in AD 349, the basilica was enriched over the centuries, but its structure remained unchanged until the 15th century, when Pope Nicholas V Parentucelli (1447-1455) decided to restore it and have the apsidal section enlarged.

The work was interrupted on the death of Nicholas V, only to be resumed with a radically new design in 1506. This was commissioned by Julius II Della Rovere (1503-1513) to Bramante, who conceived a Christian temple modelled on the Pantheon.

Gian Lorenzo Bernini, St. Peter's Square, 1667, aerial view.

Carlo Maderno, façade of St. Peter's Basilica, 1607-1614.

In 1514, following the death of both the pope and Bramante, responsibility for the work passed to Raphael, with the collaboration of Giuliano da Sangallo, and then in 1532 to Baldassare Peruzzi. Finally Michelangelo went back to Bramante's design of a Greek-cross building, but surmounted it with a large dome, rivaling the one Brunelleschi had built for Santa Maria del Fiore in Florence. Appointed architect of the Fabbrica di San Pietro in 1546 by Paul III Farnese (1534-1549), Michelangelo too worked on it until his death in 1564, after which his design was completed by Vignola, Domenico Fontana and Giacomo Della Porta. The dome was finished by Della Porta in 1590. Between 1607 and 1614, Carlo Maderno altered the layout of the basilica again, transforming Michelangelo's central plan into a longitudinal one, with the addition of three chapels on each side. While sticking to the highly monumental character Michelangelo had given the church, Maderno revealed himself to be a sensitive interpreter of its overall expressive quality in the spatial cadences of the great nave and in the handling of the façade. With its long succession of columns and pilasters, the façade has a slow rhythm that is discretely animated by slight projections in the central part and shallow recesses at the ends. Restored on the occasion of the Jubilee in 2000, the façade has regained its pinkish tone, something that has prompted quite unjustified criticism. To correct the markedly horizontal lines of Maderno's façade, Bernini initially designed two campaniles, which were never completed, and then the celebrated elliptical colonnade which, split into two arms, symbolizes the Church's embrace of the faithful and at the same time realizes the dynamic and theatrical conception of space that was typical of the Baroque. Bernini also intervened in the more sacred parts of the building and, over thirty years of activity, with a ten-year break during the pontificate of Innocent X Pamphilj (1644-1655), handled

the immense space of the basilica and the square in front of it with great skill and ingenuity. At the center of the vast square stands an obelisk, over 25 meters high. Brought to Rome from Alexandria in Egypt in AD 37 by Caligula, who had it erected in his circus, the obelisk stood alongside the Constantine's Basilica from the 4th century onward. In 1586 Sixtus V Peretti (1585-1590) decided to move the obelisk to the center of the square, in front of the basilica, and had it set on top of four bronze lions, the work of Prospero Antichi. At the sides of the obelisk stand two fountains, one designed by Maderno and the other by Bernini: the northern one was commissioned to Carlo Maderno in 1614 by Paul V Borghese (1605-1621) as a replacement for an older fountain built in 1490 by Innocent VIII Cybo (1484-1492), while the southern was added by Bernini in 1667, at the time of the layout of the square, but inaugurated only ten years later when the Acqua Paola, insufficient to supply two fountains, was supplemented with a flow of 1000 ounces of water from Lake Bracciano. Innocent's fountain, which consisted of a base with three steps supporting a round basin on which stood a baluster with a smaller bowl surmounted by an ornate pediment with three putti, was demolished by Maderno to make way for one that was larger but constructed along the same lines. In the middle of a broad mixtilinear basin stood an octagonal base, adorned with the eagle and coat of arms of Paul V, supporting a large marble bowl into which water flowed plentifully from the upper, reversed bowl, where seven powerful jets gushed a total of 300 ounces of water. A half century later Bernini moved Maderno's fountain to bring it into line with the obelisk, lowering and enlarging its basin, and constructed another, symmetrical fountain on the opposite side of the square, on whose base the crest of Pope Clement X Altieri (1670-1676) alternated with a pair of dolphins with interlaced tails.

Façade of St. Peter's Basilica, details.

Fountain of the Pigna

The upper part of the Belvedere Courtyard is named "Cortile della Pigna" after the huge bronze pinecone which was placed there by Maderno in 1607, flanked by two peacocks with which it had originally stood inside an aedicule in the courtyard known as the "Paradiso" in front of the old St. Peter's Basilica. The presence of a fountain consisting of an aedicule supported by four columns in the Paradiso Courtyard is documented from the 4th century. Later the number of columns was raised to eight, surmounted by an architrave adorned with two bronze peacocks facing one another and four dolphins spouting water at the corners. At an unknown date before the year 1000, a gigantic bronze pinecone, originally located in a temple dedicated to the goddess Cybele that stood near the Pantheon or more likely in the area of the Vatican itself, was placed inside the aedicule. The pinecone, which spurted water from numerous holes in its scales and from the originally truncated upper part, was set in a large square vase that collected the water. When work commenced on the façade of the new St. Peter's Basilica, the aedicule was dismantled and the pinecone set up in the upper Belvedere Courtyard, inside the so-called "Nicchione del Bramante," on top of a magnificent capital from the Baths of Severus Alexander. Erroneously attributed to Bramante, the large niche was added to the architectural backdrop created by Bramante for the Belvedere Courtyard by Pirro Ligorio in 1562. Behind the pinecone stands a large base decorated with figures, originally the pedestal of the column of Antoninus Pius, discovered at Montecitorio at the beginning of the 18th century.

Fountain of the Galera

At the foot of the Palazzetto del Belvedere is set the Fountain of the Galera, attributed to the Flemish artist Jan van Santen and constructed in 1618-1620 for Paul V Borghese (1605-1621). Van Santen liked to build small models of buildings, furniture and other things, earning himself the nickname "Giovanni degli studioli." The bronze fountain is a small-scale reproduction of a 17th-century galley: the masts, sails, rigging and numerous cannons that used to shoot water are represented in minute detail in this small galleon, 4-meters long.

Carlo Maderno, northern fountain in St. Peter's Square, 1614.

Gian Lorenzo Bernini, southern fountain in St. Peter's Square, 1677.

Belvedere Courtyard in the Vatican Gardens.

Jan van Santen, Fountain of the Galera in the Vatican Gardens, 1620.

Fountains of Via della Conciliazione

The need to create an easy but monumental access to St. Peter's Basilica led in the 20th century to the demolition of the dense urban fabric in the area between the Tiber embankment and St. Peter's Square and to construction of the monumental Via della Conciliazione, following the agreement reached between Church and State in 1929. The problem, tackled several times since the 15th century, had become more pressing in the 18th century, when it became necessary to render more visible Michelangelo's dome, to a great extent concealed by the structure given to the basilica by Carlo Maderno. Various plans were put forward, from Carlo Fontana's in 1694 to Giuseppe Valadier's in 1812, but it was not until 1929 that Marcello Piacentini's project, which called for the demolition of the so-called ancient quarter "spina dei borghi," was accepted. The area comprised two narrow streets, the Borgo Vecchio and the Borgo Nuovo, divided by the *spina* and terminating in the now vanished Piazza Rusticucci, from which Bernini's colonnade and St. Peter's Basilica suddenly came into view. The work, which lasted until 1950, entailed the construction of new buildings in the Fascist style along the new street, alongside the surviving structures of Palazzo Torlonia, Palazzo dei Penitenzieri and the Church of Santa Maria in Traspontina. Two 17th-century fountains in the form of aedicules constructed during the pontificate of Paul V Borghese (1605-1621) and removed from some demolished building in the area were set against the façade of the Palazzo dei Penitenzieri. The two symmetrical fountains are composed of a tympanum supported by pilasters framing a niche in which a dragon with outspread wings, emblem of the Borghese family, pours water from its mouth into a semicircular marble basin. One of the two fountains has a a smaller basin and a spread eagle, another Borghese device, in the panel of its tympanum. At the beginning of Via della Conciliazione, Piacentini, in collaboration with Attilio Spaccarelli, replaced the Neoclassical buildings of Luigi Poletti with two Fascist constructions. On the projecting part of the monumental ends of these buildings are located twin fountains surmounted by pairs of columns set side by side and crowned by an attic decorated with the coats of arms of Pope Pius XII Pacelli (1939-1958) and the Municipality of Rome.

Fountain of Via della Conciliazione, early 17th century.

Marcello Piacentini, building of the Fascist period with a fountain in Via della Conciliazione.

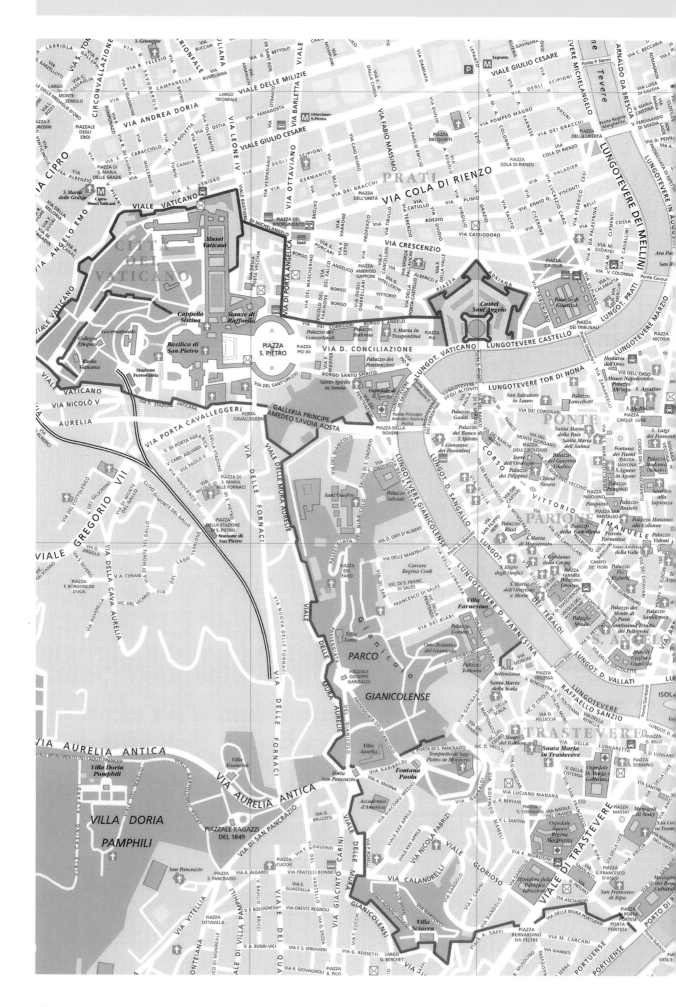

Graphic Coordinator
Dario Tagliabue

Page Layout
Sara De Michele

Editorial Coordinator
Virginia Ponciroli

Editing
Milena Archetti

Photo Research
Daniela Simone

Technical Coordinator
Mario Farè

Quality Control
Giancarlo Berti

Translation
Shanti Evans

www.electaweb.com

Printed in April 2007 by Artes Gráficas Toledo, S.A., Spain